HOW TO BE A

HOW
TO BE AN
IRONMAN

NASSER AL-MOHANNADI

دار جامعة حمد بن خليفة للنشر
HAMAD BIN KHALIFA UNIVERSITY PRESS

Hamad bin Khalifa University Press
P O Box 5825
Doha, Qatar

www.hbkupress.com

Cover photo: Zilu8 / Shutterstock.com

ISBN: 978-9927129056

Qatar National Library Cataloging-in-Publication (CIP)

Al-Mohannadi, Nasser, 1975- author.

How to be an ironman / by Prof. Dr. Nasser Al-Mohannadi. – Doha :

Hamad Bin Khalifa University Press , 2018.

Pages ; cm

ISBN: 978-9927-129-05-6

1. AL-Mohannadi, Nasser, 1975-. 2. Management -- Qatar. 3. Work life balance. 4. Celebrities --

Qatar-- Biography. 5. Ability. 6. Ironman triathlon -- Training. II.Title.

CT1919.Q25 M64 2018

920.05363–dc23   2018 26619404

Contents

Acknowledgements

This book is not just the story of my journey to become an Ironman. It is also about the people who have joined me on the road, since this is not a journey one can make alone.

First and foremost I am grateful to God for giving me health and strength to make the journey. I would like to thank Maryam, who didn't understand why I always disappeared so early in the morning; Saqer, who didn't know why I was tired all the time; Galya, for her enduring patience, love and support, and her family for tracking me during the race; Lahdan, for his encouragement, networking and support; and all my other family members, in particular my nephew, who has taken the very first steps to becoming an Ironman himself. Many thanks also go to the other Qatari who first completed an Ironman race; Ebrahim, for being a training partner, strong competitor and friend; and two other training buddies, Johnny and Syafei.

I would definitely not have completed the journey without my coaches, especially Joseph, who became my coach after I decided to register for the African Championship. My gratitude also goes to Hossam, Eric, Bryan, Sergio and Haytham for their coaching on different elements of the triathlon and Dr Zarko, Nicol and Adrian for their help with my injuries.

I would like to thank my family and friends in Qatar, Bahrain, Kuwait, the United Arab Emirates, Oman, The Netherlands and the rest of the world, who have been strong supporters. My gratitude also goes to the Doha TriClub for providing me the opportunity to train and participate in the races they organised.

Participating in an Ironman race requires financial support or other support in kind. I would like to thank the Ministry of Sports and Culture, my trip sponsor, and the national Olympic Swimming Federation for providing a swim coach to help me master the open water swim; Aspetar hospital for support with my injuries; the sports channel ALKASS for TV coverage of my journey to become an Ironman and the Qatar National Bank for sponsoring my participation in the earlier Bahrain half Ironman.

Last but not least, I would like to thank sport in general. It has allowed me to become healthier in body and mind and developed in me positive thinking, perseverance and patience. This is what this book is about: how sport can contribute to a healthy body and mind and what we can learn from this for our daily lives.

Introduction

Once upon a time there were two friends who worked for a pearl diver. The pearl diver was a modest, hard-working and God-fearing man and he was very proud of the two boys working for him. The older boy was strong and outgoing, and always got the best price for the pearls he harvested. The younger was modest but very bright, and the pearl diver could always rely upon him. Despite their different personalities, the two friends respected each other. They complemented each other, and this made their pearl diving business one of the most successful in the village where they lived.

One day, the pearl diver realised he had not long to live. He had been diving for pearls his whole life, ever since he was a little boy. The years had taken a heavy toll on him. After dinner, when the old man was resting, he asked the two friends to join him. "God has called me, my boys," he said. The two young men looked startled. "Don't weep," said the pearl diver when he saw the tears in their eyes, "I have had a good life and God has rewarded me with you, and I am sure you will support my family and your own families. I can die in peace." The old man closed his eyes as his last breath departed from his fragile body.

The two friends followed in their teacher's footsteps. Very early in the morning they left with their boat to dive for pearls. In the afternoon, the younger one removed the pearls from their shells while the older sold the pearls at a good price.

One day, the younger of the two friends had a brilliant idea. If it was possible to stay underwater longer, they would save time and could harvest more pearls. He took the stomach of a goat, cleaned and dried it and filled it with air. Then he made a straw from a plant and inserted it into the air-filled sack. While he was working hard, he did not notice that he was being watched by an oryx, and if you looked closely, you could see the oryx smile. The younger boy went underwater and breathed the air in the goat's stomach. "It works," he declared, and immediately showed his invention to his friend. "Good work," his friend said. And indeed, the younger one's invention allowed them to harvest almost twice as many pearls as they had before.

The invention did not go unnoticed in the village and people started to ask questions. How was it possible that these two young men were so successful? It was known that the older one was a good salesman, but their growing wealth could not just be the result of his commercial skills. One Friday, after the prayer time, the villagers asked him to tell them the secret of their success. "I made a great discovery," the older one said. "I invented a way to breathe underwater. Now we can harvest almost twice as many pearls as before." The younger of the two boys heard his friend claiming he was responsible for the innovation, but kept silent. He had been taught not to speak out against someone who is older.

The two friends became very wealthy and the older one decided to expand their business. He hired many other divers from the village, equipping them all with his friend'Ts invention. Soon the whole town was working for the two friends. The harvest of pearls almost doubled and the two young men did not have to dive themselves anymore. But the younger one did not like it. At this pace of harvesting, the pearls would not have sufficient time to grow and it would not take long before they would no longer find high-quality pearls.

This time the younger one decided to speak up. If they continued like this, they would bring ruin upon the entire town. One day, at a meeting of the townsmen, he stood up and said: "My beloved friend, and dear people, we should stop using my invention to harvest pearls. If we continue harvesting at this pace, it will not be long before the sea is depleted." His friend raged in anger and shouted: "How dare you stand up against me, even though I am older than you are? And how dare you claim that this is your invention? Go, leave this town. You are no longer welcome here!" "Yes," said the men present. "How dare he?" And they turned their backs on him.

The younger boy went into the desert. As he was very bright, he managed to survive in the barren conditions. At night he slept in a cave. During the day he managed to grow some vegetables, having designed an irrigation system, and hunted wild goats with hand-made weapons. One evening, when he had not been very successful at hunting, he was astonished to see what looked like an oryx appearing before him. "I must be delusional," he said to himself, "because of lack of food today. And what's this? It seems as if the oryx is weeping." The animal's tears fell onto the dry sand. The boy realised that he should be patient and his perseverance would eventually pay off. Although it appeared that everyone had turned their backs on him, God certainly hadn't, and the oryx was a sign which strengthened this belief.

Meanwhile, in the village people continued harvesting pearls as if nothing had happened. The older boy became even wealthier, as he no longer had to share with his younger friend. However, not long afterwards the divers observed that the pearls they were harvesting were getting smaller and smaller, and the older boy could no longer get a good price for them. Eventually, they didn't find any pearls at all. It was then that they began to realise the younger boy might have been right. For a while, the people could live on their large monetary reserves, since they had accumulated much wealth over time. But it did not take long before their reserves were depleted and the divers were no longer able to feed themselves and their families. Even the older boy, the wealthiest in town, and his family were starving.

One Friday, after the prayer time, the people gathered in the centre of the town, lamenting and praying. They thought God had forsaken them. Then suddenly an oryx appeared. Fire came from his eyes. His breath was heavy. To the astonishment of all the people gathered there, the oryx started to speak: "People," he said, "you have brought this misery upon yourselves, as you have been blinded by greed." Then he turned to the older of the two friends: "You are the worst of all. You not only discarded the advice of your beloved friend, you also lied about his invention, claiming it was yours." And then the older one recognised the eyes of the old pearl diver they had been working for and who had more or less raised him. He fell on his knees and started to weep. "Go into the desert and look for your friend," the oryx said. "If you are lucky, he will not kill you."

So the older boy did. After seven days and seven nights he found his friend. He hardly recognised him. He had lost a lot of weight and his hair and skin were covered in dust. He had almost taken on the colour of the sand surrounding them. The older one fell on his knees, told him what had happened, and asked him not to kill him. "I will take your place in the desert if you want me to," he said, with tears in his eyes. "You should lead the people of our village out of their misery." "Why did you lie?" the younger friend asked him. "Because I was jealous of you," he replied. "I was afraid you would challenge my position in our town, after your great invention." "Stand up," the younger one said and reached out his hand. "You will not take my place in the desert. Nor will I kill you. The old pearl diver, who was like a father to us and a God-fearing man, has taught us to forgive. And that's what I will do. Let us both go back to the town and try to salvage what your greed and my invention have done."

So they did. They decided to destroy all the goat stomachs and a law was passed forbidding their use for harvesting pearls. After a short while, the pearls started to grow again and the people resumed their old life, living happily ever after. And outside the town on a small rock stood the oryx, smiling again.

* * *

This book is about my journey, which began in the late 1980s – and even before - on the Arabian Peninsula, a journey to achieve a childhood dream.

I am not special, at least not more than any other human being. Nor am I gifted with miraculous physical powers, like the Marvel Comics hero Ironman, which might help me complete the toughest race on earth. True, I have been lucky. I have good health and was born into a family which benefited from the economic growth and development of my country, Qatar. But I am not a professional athlete. Although I have always liked sport, it is only one part of my life, and my parents never particularly encouraged me in that area. I am married with a busy social life, involving friends and a large extended family. Family values are an important element of my culture. I graduated with a PhD in engineering from a prestigious university and have a busy and responsible job, working in the energy sector in an oil and gas company. I am also an adjunct professor at University in Doha. In other words, the journey I took is for anyone.

This is also the journey of a country, the State of Qatar. A country that began as a poor, backward and insignificant part of the world, where people struggled for their basic needs under harsh conditions, and is now the richest country in the world in terms of GDP per capita, following the discovery of oil and gas reserves in the 1940s. But nothing should be taken for granted, as this journey will teach us. The dark side of economic growth and a rapid increase in wealth is complacency and an unhealthy lifestyle. The pearl divers and fishers of Qatar did not suffer the obesity or diabetes of today's generation. The challenges ahead for Qatar are manifold. The country is located in a region suffering from political, military and religious upheavals and is dependent on one major source of income, the exploitation of oil and gas.

Finally, this book is about the journey of every individual. We all face our Ironman race, either because we want to achieve a dream or because we are confronted with difficult circumstances in our lives. In other words, this book is not just about attaining the fitness to complete an arduous sports event, but also about acquiring an iron soul - being disciplined, committed, positive and persistent. Our life is a continuous struggle to become an Ironman and to declare victory after we have crossed the finish line. This book will appeal to readers interested in a human story, as well as those facing the personal and professional challenges of life.

Sport, or any kind of physical exercise, is an interesting phenomenon. The first human beings on this planet had no need to engage in it. Physical exercise was part of the daily struggle to survive. They swam to catch fish or, in Qatar, they dived to harvest pearls. They ran to catch animals to eat, or to escape being eaten by ferocious beasts. Obesity did not exist in those days. Every man had well-shaped abdominal muscles, or what is commonly known nowadays as a six-pack. The weak became a prey. Physical exercise also played a role in the defence of land, which was at the heart of warfare. In fact, the history of sport may go back as far as the earliest military training, as a means to determine whether individuals were fit and useful for service. Team sports may have been developed to train and prove the capability to fight and work together as a team, in the army for instance. The history of sport can teach us both about social changes and the nature of sport itself.

Some historians claim that team sports as we know them today are an invention of Western culture. British Prime Minister John Major said in 1995: "We invented the majority of the world's great sports...19th century Britain was the cradle of a leisure revolution every bit as significant as the agricultural and industrial revolutions we launched in the century before." Traditional team sports are seen as originating from Britain before being exported across the British Empire. European colonialism certainly helped spread particular games around the world. The modern Olympic Games were initially Europe-dominated and when similar games around the world were merged, rules were standardised along European lines. The Industrial Revolution and mass production brought increased leisure time in which to play or observe spectator sports, as well as greater accessibility to sports of many kinds.

Sport, as with all kinds of games, is a microcosm of real life, and many lessons can be learned from it. A football coach once said that he used to shout at the players when he observed they had not been communicating sufficiently with each other on the field. Team sports teach us the importance of working together and the power of good communication. Scoring a goal is much easier when team members play together, check who is well positioned in the field and to whom the ball can be passed.

The roots of the Ironman competition are in Hawaii. The idea for the original Ironman triathlon came during the awards ceremony for the 1977 O'ahu Perimeter Relay. Athletes had been debating who were the fittest: runners, cyclists or swimmers. It was decided that the debate should be settled through a race combining the three existing long-distance competitions already on Hawaii: the Waikiki Roughwater Swim (3.86 km), the Around-Oahu Bike Race (185.07 km) and the Honolulu Marathon (42.195 km). Prior to racing, each athlete received three sheets of paper listing a few rules and a course description. Handwritten on the last page was this exhortation: "Swim 2.4 miles! Bike 112 miles! Run 26.2 miles! Brag for the rest of your life." The event organiser declared: "Whoever finishes first, we'll call him the Ironman." Of the fifteen men to start off in the early morning of February 18, 1978, twelve completed the race, and the first to earn the title Ironman completed the course with a time of 11 hours, 46 minutes, 58 seconds.

Since this first Ironman race in 1978, Ironman has developed into a worldwide phenomenon. Every year, half and full Ironman races are organised across the globe, culminating in the World Championship in Kona, Hawaii. Only the best Ironman athletes compete in this last battle.

Over the years, Ironman events have become more commercial. This is true for most top level sports and without commercial sponsorship, top sport would not have reached its current level. Commercial promotion also allows the public to enjoy sporting performances and to dream about becoming athletes themselves. This is what triggered me to embark on my journey.

This book is structured as follows: in the first two chapters, I will describe the journey that took me to racing day, 10th April 2016, the day of the African Ironman Championship in Port Elizabeth. The journey towards this day is just as important, maybe even more so, than the Ironman race itself. The first chapter deals with the early years of planning (1988-2014), when I gradually developed a strategy to achieve my goal. The second chapter (2015-2016) deals with the implementation of this strategy and preparations for the African Ironman Championship. The next three chapters describe the race in detail: swimming, biking and running. But the story does not end there. As an engineer, I know the importance of evaluating projects and learning lessons. Hence, the last chapter of this book is about the way forward. How has participating in an Ironman race contributed to my future life?

The story of my journey and the lessons that can be drawn from it are intertwined, making the book accessible to both types of readers: those who would like to read a personal story about an individual pursuing his dream and those who want to read a book that, hopefully, adds value to their personal life or career. I hope you will find this book both enjoyable and informative.

Chapter 1

The Journey
Strategy and Planning (1988-2014)

Looking back...

As I waited for the start of the Ironman race in Port Elizabeth, South Africa, on 10th April 2016, I focused on what lay ahead of me. It would turn out to be a test of endurance lasting more than 14 hours.

I did not think about the long road I had travelled to reach this point. It had been tough but also rewarding, a journey of peaks and troughs. When I had explained to people what I was doing, they often looked at me in disbelief. "You will be covering the distance from Doha to Hofuf (AL-Hasa), in the Eastern Province of Saudi Arabia, about 240 kilometres non-stop," my father exclaimed when I told him what the Ironman race entailed.

But the Ironman race is not so different from the journey made by all of us, called life, with its highs and lows, moments of ecstatic happiness and of deep sorrow. So don't be too impressed by my sporting achievement and be proud of your journey as well. I am just sharing with you lessons I have learned, which can be applied to everyone in their personal or professional lives, to individuals and organisations. There are too many testimonies of Ironman athletes about "me, myself and I." This book is ultimately not about me. It's a book about and for all of you who travel a journey called life.

... to my childhood years.

My journey started when I was 12 years old. I was born in 1975 in Doha, Qatar, at a time when Doha was unrecognisable compared to what it is now. There were no high-rise buildings and what is now Doha's West Bay, filled with office towers, hotels and shopping malls, was a plain with a few houses, next to the sea. I was born into a local family, one of the tribes which had settled on the Qatari peninsula. My ancestors originate from Al Thakhira, a village on the east coast of Qatar with, nowadays, about 14,000 inhabitants.

My father was born in 1940, not long after the discovery of oil in the late 1930s in Dukhan. In those days, the country, still a British protectorate, was poor and people led simple lives from our current perspective, but their lives were perhaps richer than ours today. Nothing was taken for granted in a society where people made a living from catching fish or diving for pearls. Men were often months away, out on the sea, while women took care of the children.

My grandfather, a pearl diver, died before my father was born and my grandmother died shortly after his birth. His uncle raised my father, who worked as a shepherd and assistant boy on a pearl diving boat. He would never have any education as a child. After the discovery of oil, he took a basic job in the country's young oil industry. In this period he also learned English and got a job in the Qatari public sector, in the area of foreign trade. And the apple doesn't fall far from the tree – in those days my father was also in charge of the Al Thakhira sports club. After his early retirement, he established his own business, which was successful and still exists today, co-managed by my brother and myself.

The journey of Qatar

Qatar is a country on the Arabian peninsula with approximately 2.2 million inhabitants, of which only 20% of the population are Qataris. In terms of GDP per capita, Qatar is the richest country in the world, followed by Luxembourg and Singapore. The country has been on an amazing journey, particularly during the last century.

At the beginning of the 20th century, Qatar had only about 10,000 inhabitants. From the mid 16th century until the First World War, the country was part of the Ottoman empire. At the beginning of the Great War, it became a British protectorate. The country became fully independent in 1971. Qatar is ruled by the Al Thani family.

Qatar's economic growth is linked to the discovery of oil. The country started exporting oil in the late 1940s. Currently, 60% of GDP comes from the oil and gas industry. Qatar has one of the largest gas reserves worldwide (12% of global reserves), concentrated in the so-called Northern Field. In 2008, the government launched the Qatar National Vision 2030 (QNV), which aims to "transform Qatar into an advanced society capable of achieving sustainable development" by 2030. The plan's development goals are divided into four central pillars: economic, social, human and environmental development. An important objective of the QNV is to diversify the economy and reduce the country's dependency on oil and gas.

Qatar has invested substantially in the development of sport. It is the only country in the world which has declared a National Sports Day, in early February each year, promoting a healthy mind in a healthy body.

In many ways I resemble my father, who is one of my great examples in life. He liked travelling and exploring and was, certainly for his time and generation, open-minded and independent. He got on easily with the first foreigners who started working in the country. His childhood was far from easy and he has always worked very hard to see his family prosper. It was my father who taught me that you can realise your dreams, but only if you work hard enough. And it was from my mother that I learned the importance of planning. I am deeply indebted to my parents for teaching me the valuable lesson that 'larks don't fall ready roasted.'

I grew up in a quiet neighbourhood of Doha, the youngest of six siblings. I have one older brother, followed by three older sisters, of whom two have passed away. I was the fifth child of my parents, with one younger sister coming after me. The death of my sisters has shaped my parents' life and made them more protective, especially towards my younger sister and me.

I liked sport and in those days it was primarily football, as this was the only sport people really appreciated and enjoyed. I learned to play when I was five years old. My parents were wary of any sport that might cause serious injuries. I still remember buying a skateboard and practicing standing on it in the tiny bathroom of the house we were then living in. When my father found out, he asked me to return it. It was far too dangerous. "Safety first," he said. This attitude has made me a risk-averse person and I am still aware of this when I am biking or swimming. It probably explains why I didn't tell my parents about my preparations and the race itself until I had completed it successfully. "Why are you always yawning?" my father would ask in the final months before the race, when I was training twice a day. Since we live on a family compound, my mother found out that I often left the house very early in the morning to train - a necessity in the extreme hot weather of Qatar. She threatened to slash the tyres of my car if I left so early again.

Being risk-averse is also a positive thing. Becoming an Ironman is about pushing your limits, but pushing them too far can lead to setbacks, like serious injuries. In other words, "safety first" is an important piece of advice to anybody who wants to embark upon a similar journey. Despite being wary of taking too many risks, I still made many mistakes, which I will mention later.

But it was not just my parents' fear of 'dangerous' sports which stopped me from playing anything but football. During my childhood, it was the only sport that got serious attention. Most other sports seemed to be from a different planet. It is interesting that the people of a country on a peninsula surrounded by the Arabian Gulf and inhabited by former pearl divers showed no interest in swimming. Historically, the sea had been a source of life, but not for recreation or physical exercise. Although the country is virtually flat - the highest elevation is a mere 103 metres above sea level - yet nobody ran or biked.

Camels were the usual means of transportation. Of course the harsh climate, especially during the summer, did not help. So football it was. I played it in every street, alley or square of our neighbourhood. Often I played barefoot, injuring my feet, and had to promise my mother, who more than once had to bandage me up, that I would wear shoes the next time I played. I admit I did not always obey her.

From a local Qatari boy...

It was 1988 and I was 12 years old when I first saw an Ironman race on a small television set at home. I still remember it vividly. It was a short item in the sports coverage, following the regular news. I remember the alien-looking tall men wearing bathing caps and goggles, waiting for the race to start. From that moment on, the images were burned into my mind: men and women choosing to swim 3.8 kilometres, bike 180 kilometres and, if that were not enough, run a full marathon of 42.2 kilometres. It was and is the most arduous of all sports. I vividly remember what I felt – that I wanted to do the same one day.

I went to school in Doha and I daresay I was a bright student. Most people have always thought of me as a typical nerd, his head in books, and some of them were very surprised when they discovered my interest and accomplishments in sport. From my youth through to adulthood, I tried to balance my studies and love for sport. I learned early on how important the work-life balance is and how sport helps maintain this.

Oil and gas have made Qatar into one of the most affluent countries in the world. At the same time, the country has developed the typical "diseases" that go hand in hand with economic development, such as unhealthy lifestyles. Working hours have increased and so have the pressures on people: to perform, or buy as big a house or car as one's neighbour. "Work never finishes," I tend to say. One of the best books I have read on this subject is Robin Sharma's "The Monk Who Sold his Ferrari":

"There we were, two slaves to the clock, toiling away on the sixty-fourth floor of some steel and glass monolith while most sane people were at home with their families, thinking we had the world by the tail, blinded by an illusionary version of success."

Family used to be the cornerstone of our society and this has rapidly changed in the wake of economic development, as people have no time anymore to spend with their kin. Life has turned into a rat race with little time and appreciation for pursuing dreams. Especially in such an environment, striking a healthy balance between work and leisure is extremely important. And sport also contributes to a healthy lifestyle, preventing obesity and related diseases.

It is important, in this context, to refer to another characteristic, at the root of Islamic philosophy: modesty. I was always told not to brag about my accomplishments. Maybe it was fear of the "evil eye" that might be put on you if you were too successful. But it definitely also goes back to the knowledge of where my family and tribe have come from and the desire never to forget our roots and ancestry. Being the perceived underdog is a powerful starting position, not only in sports but also in business. Being the winner also raises expectations and, very often, increases pressure. Unfortunately, modesty is no longer valued by younger generations, probably also under the influence of the "Americanisation" of our culture. Modesty appears to be more a trait of the east than of the west.

I never stood out and people appeared not to notice me, at least not at first. I still remember a football tournament organised at high school by an uncle of His Highness, the current emir, when our team was the underdog. Eventually, we reached second place in the tournament, although I had not been able to play in the final myself as I was away for a science competition. In the quarter final against the current emir's uncle's team – it was 2:2 – I scored the winning goal. I still remember being carried around on the shoulders of my team members. It was a formidable feeling for an underdog.

After finishing high school, I went to university in Oman. As I had an uncle who was a surgeon, my family thought it would be a good idea if I studied medicine as well, and at school I did well in science and maths. I received a scholarship to study in Oman. However, I soon found out that medicine was not an appropriate choice for me. I didn't like it at all, and even now I cannot stand the sight of blood. So before it was too late, I decided to switch to petroleum engineering. My brother had advised me to do this, since Qatar's economy had become dependent on the oil and gas industry.

Actually, I had always wanted to become a pilot, like many boys of my age. I liked aviation and travelling, and was very fond of geography. As a kid I could spend hours studying an atlas and even fall asleep on it. My love for geography was one of the reasons I started to travel, following in the footsteps of my father. I have so far visited 121 countries. As regards becoming a pilot, my father soon disenchanted me: "a pilot is nothing more than a bus driver," he said, and I followed his advice and switched to engineering.

...121 countries

Another of my ambitions is to travel and visit as many countries as possible. Saint Augustine said, "The world is a book and those who do not travel, read only one page." I visited my 121st country in the autumn of 2017, the honour going to Malta, the last country in Europe I had not visited yet. Travelling has enabled me to experience the diversity of our world, in terms of nature, culture, religion, wealth and people. Through travelling you learn to put things in perspective. At the same time, it has given me the opportunity to enlighten people about my home country and culture, as I have tried to be, at least informally, an ambassador of Qatar.

... to a world citizen and explorer.

After my graduation and a year of work experience in Qatar, I decided to do my master's degree and PhD in the United States. I had been to the States before and felt attracted to the country, and the university was renowned. It took me six years to complete my studies there. In the last months, before the defence of my dissertation, I got married.

"History repeats," they say. Just as I had done at school in Doha and at university in Oman, I played football in Colorado. Again, I was the underdog, being put in the reserve team, Team B. However, during the play-offs our team won against the main team, Team A, and I scored the winning goal. Once more, I scored a critical goal in the quarter final of the tournament, like all those years before in Doha. It was a crazy moment, and this time we won the school championship.

My time in Colorado was of pivotal importance for my

development. I changed from a typical Qatari young man into a world citizen, an explorer. My worldview changed dramatically. Having come from an environment in which much was impossible, difficult or dangerous, I started to experiment and became more open-minded. I no longer confined myself to football, but began to learn skiing, snowboarding, skateboarding and indoor climbing. All of that was not easy for a young man who had been told not to get involved in dangerous activities. I learned to play the guitar and even got my motorbike driving license. My interest in food also developed in that period. Up until then, I had only known local Arabic or Indian food, besides the typical fast food which is almost unavoidable when living in the United States. In Colorado, I learned to appreciate the diversity of what the culinary world has to offer. I learned to eat sushi, for instance. If somebody had told me, years before, that I would eat raw fish, I would have said he was mad.

Two other characteristics of my personality were revealed when I was in Colorado and they played a vital role in my journey to become an Ironman.

First, I am a very independent person. I do not go with the flow. Unlike my fellow students from the middle east, I enjoyed mingling with locals, and when it came to sport or joint projects at university, I was a team player. But part of me also craved solitude from time to time, and I was determined to make my own destiny. Some people in those times would probably have called me selfish or egocentric. And maybe I was to some extent, but the rough edges of this character trait disappeared after I went back to Doha. Yet I still have a deep desire to be an independent person.

Second, the exploratory phase I went through in Colorado triggered another part of my personality; that I feel and want to be different from others and, preferably, be the first to have had a certain experience. I have been to countries no Qatari would ever dream of visiting and I wanted to be one of the first Qataris to finish an Ironman race, just as I was one of the first to run a full marathon. In the same vein, I like healthy competition. Perhaps I was following in the footsteps of my father, who struggled and rose above what was and still is common in his home town, Al Thakhira.

After I obtained my PhD, my wife and I moved back to Doha, where I started teaching at the university. Not long afterwards, I began working for an international oil company (IOC), while continuing my university lecturing. After six and a half years at IOC, I was asked to head the Research and Technology Department of the national energy company, a position that I held for a few years until the Department was closed down in the wake of the declining oil price. Immediately after that, I was asked to work on a project for the European central bank dealing with climate change and energy, and was seconded to a joint venture energy company, in charge of operations in the northern gas field of Qatar, the largest gas field in the world.

Contemplating building a house…

All this time, the images I had seen on television back in 1988 were on the back burner of my mind, until early 2015 when I made the decision to do an Ironman race.

One can compare this process with building a house. Before you actually buy the ground and start to construct it, you ask yourself: where do I want to live? What should the house look like? What materials do I want to use? In business one would refer to it as strategy and planning.

This is what I did in this first part of my journey to become an Ironman. Besides playing football constantly, I gradually improved my skills in swimming, biking and running, mostly by trial and error. I didn't tell anybody what I was doing and maybe I didn't know myself exactly what I was aiming for.

After 1988, I focused on the different elements of a triathlon, until the pieces came together in early 2015 and I started to build my house.

Strategy and Planning (1988-2014)

- 1988: watched Ironman on TV
- 2006: learned to run
- 2007: learned to swim breast stroke
- 2008: 3 km run (competition)
- 2009: 10 km run (competition) and 5 km breast stroke (challenge)
- 2011: marathon Tromso (Norway)
- 2012: knee injury; bought first road bike and first long ride during 1st national sports day with Dr. Mohd J., Ali M. and Saoud J. Al Kuwari as founders of Qatar cyclist
- 2013: groin and shoulder injury
- 2014: learned to swim freestyle
- 2015: 100 km bike ride

While it took me just 14 hours from the start of the race in Port Elizabeth to the finish line, to get to the starting point was a journey of more than 27 years. Maybe this goes with my personality, the man who needs time to get to grips with things, the underdog who then surfaces. In early 2015, when I started to train with Ebrahim and Johnny, we gave each other nicknames. I was 'the turtle'. I was definitely not the fastest of the three. However, when it came to perseverance and persistence, I stood out. I never quit.

Preparation is necessary before undertaking an Ironman

race. As a matter of fact, preparation is everything. Crucially, an extended time of preparation allows you to make mistakes. And I made many. But we do not learn from our achievements in life, but mainly from our mistakes.

I started by observing how others were swimming, biking or running. I learned how to float in the water but had no idea how to move and which techniques to use. As a child, I had a BMX bike, but biking a long distance was a completely different story. And I knew how to run on the football field, chasing the ball, or to run away from a bully, but not how to run long distance. So I watched others doing it and started to copy them. Looking back, 60% to 70% of my skills I learned by myself, and the people I met during the first part of my journey taught me the rest. They were not professional coaches or professional athletes. Most of the time they were amateurs whom I encountered and I simply asked them questions. This is how I learned breaststroke. I saw a man in the pool doing it and asked him what I should do. "Breath in, head in the water, out again, and breath out and in," he said. I used this technique for years before learning freestyle swimming, which I found extremely difficult to master.

During this process, it was helpful that I was no longer afraid to experiment, although the words of my parents resonated in the back of my head, and they still do. Working for an international company was also useful, as I had many expatriate colleagues for whom swimming, biking and running were not alien sports.

One man in particular was very important for me, Oliver Seybold. He now lives in Brazil and is a great lover of dogs. He has twelve. I am rather scared of them and was therefore an easy victim for his pranks. Oliver was 47 when we met and a very good athlete. Swimming and running were his secret, he always said. He pushed me to go beyond my limits.

Once in 2009, he challenged me while we were swimming: "Let's see who can do most laps." Oliver was fast and swam freestyle, which I had not yet mastered. He did 200 laps in the pool and got out, while I was still only on about 100 laps. After a while, he came back to find me still swimming. "You can stop now," he said. But I continued until I had finished 208 laps. It took me about four hours. Yes, the nickname turtle suited me well.

... and learning from my mistakes.

Late in the first decade of this century, I had the idea of doing a marathon. But first I wanted to experience running over a longer distance in a competition, so I participated in my first running competition, in Doha in 2008, covering a distance of 3 kilometres. A year later, in 2009, I participated in a competition involving a 10 kilometre run.

In January 2011, after a colleague at IOC had run a marathon, I made up my mind to do the same. I felt a lack of challenge at work, so decided I should have a shot at the marathon of Tromso, Norway. If I succeeded, I would be one of the first Qataris to have run a marathon. Norway was one of the countries I had not visited at that point and I was looking forward to experiencing the famous midsummer. I would run the marathon with a friend, who unfortunately had to cancel in the end, as he could not train, but he joined me anyway to provide moral support. Big thanks to Mohammed for that. The marathon would take place in June of that year. This meant that I would have to train in the spring, when temperatures in Doha can be very high. So the timing of my decision was not ideal. Still, I was very committed and took my running shoes with me wherever I went. I also downloaded a training schedule from the Internet, which I followed conscientiously. But then I noticed that the distances indicated in the plan were not in miles but in kilometres, so I had consistently been training distances that were too short. Increasing my "mileage" by 60% to reach the actual levels was simply too much. During the last training run before the marathon, I fainted. As I had never heard of massage, warming-up, cooling-down or recovery, I also developed knee problems two weeks before the marathon, the result of extremely tight muscles.

Norway is definitely one of the most beautiful countries I have ever visited and the scenery we ran through was like a midsummer night's dream. Before the start, I had written down the names of people close to me on my arm. Looking at their names would help me endure the suffering. I ran the first 20 kilometres of the marathon without any difficulties, but the next 15 kilometres were very tough. Tromso is situated in a beautiful area, covered with mountains and lakes, but I had not made the effort to study the route of the marathon properly. I had no idea it would take us through such a hilly area. However, in the last few kilometres I recovered and managed to finish at the same pace at which I had started. I even caught up with some other runners who had passed me earlier. But after the race, I neglected the necessary aftercare and recovery process. I didn't see the need for a massage, for instance, and went back immediately to the hotel and had dinner. As a result, I suffered a lot the following week and could hardly walk.

In December of 2011, in the aftermath of the marathon, I started to develop multiple injuries, all of them on the left side of my body. My left knee started to hurt, as well as my left shoulder and left toe. But the biggest problem I had during the next three years was an injury in my left groin. For a while I used to visit the hospital three times a week and I tried every possible treatment, from acupuncture to visiting a chiropractor, whose remedies were painful and made me scared of going to the next appointment.

In early 2012, I had to give up football, my favourite sport at the time. I have never regained my football skills completely and have only very recently started to play again, in a very easygoing way. It was one of my heroes, the Dutch football player Johan Cruyff, who said that every disadvantage has its advantage. My injuries from the marathon in Norway seemed to be frustrating my ambitions, but it was actually the reverse, although I didn't realise it then.

First, I learned a lot from the mistakes I had made, like poor preparation and aftercare. These lessons were crucial for the next part of my journey, which started in early 2015.

Second, since I had to give up football completely, I began preparing for the Ironman race.

Last but not least, it helped a lot that my physiotherapist, Nicol, was at that time, coincidentally, training for a half Ironman race. His wife even participated in a full Ironman race. This inspired me to continue my quest, despite all the difficulties. During 2014, I gradually recovered and in the end I managed to do a full Ironman race even before he did, in his home country, South Africa.

During this difficult period of my life, doing any kind of serious sport was out of the question. I could not swim, bike or run. I only trained using fitness equipment. Especially during Ramadan, when we tend to eat too much, physical problems and pain tended to be aggravated. I was not happy. Yet I never really contemplated giving up and becoming a couch potato, watching television at home. Sport was too dear to me, nor was it in my turtle nature to give in.

The Ironman race was still a prime time show playing in my mind and dreams. With the race in mind, in 2012 I bought my first road bike. Although I still couldn't run or play football with my knee injury, I could ride a bike for short distances. It seemed too heavy and large for my small build, until one of my colleagues taught me how to ride it, along with terms like 'cadence' (number of full cycles taken within a minute by the pair of feet) which until then were like Chinese to me.

Later, in 2013 and 2014, when my injuries were gradually healing, I learned freestyle swimming. I saw an Australian man swimming laps in the sea outside the Four Seasons Hotel in Doha. I asked him if I could join him and we decided to swim together once a week. This was when I began to master the technique of freestyle swimming. How I would like to swim with him again now, just to see if he is still faster than me.

There are two important lessons I draw from this period and the laundry list of mistakes that I made.

First, when embarking upon such an extreme journey – in my case the marathon – do not try to reinvent the wheel. Ask advice from the right people. My independence did not always serve me well. I believed I could prepare for a marathon by myself, just by watching people or browsing the Internet, but I missed many essentials. During training, for example, I only cared about endurance and running long distances. I didn't know that it is also important to develop speed and strength. Nor had it occurred to me that success in an endurance sport also requires healthy and balanced nutrition.

Most of our strengths are often also our pitfalls and weaknesses. My independence and urge to be different or be first to do something new, helped me a lot during my journey. At the same time, independence can turn into stubborn and selfish behaviour, the feeling that you can master every problem by yourself and don't have to listen to good advice. I know I can be like this sometimes and this is what happened before and after the marathon in Norway.

A second lesson is that training for an Ironman race involves training for all elements of the triathlon simultaneously. One of the reasons my preparatory period before 2014 was quite long, was that I had acquired the skills needed for an Ironman race separately, but had not put them together. The building blocks of my Lego house were all around me, but I had not started to assemble them. In 2009, I was swimming 5 kilometres, more than the distance of a full Ironman race, but I only started biking long distances in the spring of 2015. Only then did I ride my first 100 kilometres, and I needed more than four days to recover from it. In 2011, I had put all my efforts into training for the marathon, almost forgetting about swimming and biking. Good Ironman training involves a balanced training schedule, practicing all the three disciplines.

Eventually, 'time heals all wounds' and towards the end of 2014, I was more or less fully recovered. Now it was time to start building my house and prepare for the Ironman race.

Chapter 2

The Journey
Execution (2015-2016)

Starting to build my house

In January 2015, I started to build my house. It would be finished on 10th April 2016, much earlier than I had expected.

Various things triggered me to start building. As mentioned, the post-marathon injuries were wearing off and giving up football made it easier to focus completely on the triathlon. But perhaps even more important was the drive I felt to do something that would give me positive energy. My mother's health was poor at that time and I was quite worried. Also, my company was increasingly coming under pressure, due to the gradually declining oil price. In the late spring of 2015, a decision was made to restructure it. From a professional point of view, this was not an easy time for me, but at least the new role meant more time to train.

In February 2015, I participated in my first "public" triathlon, sprint distance, i.e. a 500 metre swim, a 20 kilometre bike ride and a 5 kilometre run. It was during this race that I met Ebrahim, later dubbed "the rabbit," as he was easily the fastest member of what would later become our training "gang." Our first encounter was in the swimming pool, lane no. 9. It was a "rolling start," every five seconds, and he was in the same lane.

He greeted me in Arabic and I immediately noticed the Qatari dialect. I was intrigued, as I had not expected another local to participate in the triathlon. We did not have much time to talk; he was indeed as fast as a rabbit. However, after the race we decided to train together. For this purpose, we joined the Doha TriClub in March 2015.

Our next goal would be to take part in a triathlon at the Doha Pearl, one of the city's renowned and prestigious extensions into the sea, crowded with luxurious hotels, restaurants and apartments. Qataris may not be the best swimmers, but they sure know how to make use of the sea! It would be my first Olympic distance triathlon: a 1.5 kilometre swim, 40 kilometre bike race, and a 10 kilometre run. On the eve of the race, we met Johnny, an English expatriate working at the Four Seasons Hotel, who was interested in joining us. He had seen me training intensively at the Four Seasons and was curious to find out why. The hotel was one of my favourite locations for training and exercise. His mother was an athlete herself, a former runner in the UK national cross-country team.

After the Pearl triathlon, we joined together with a common goal - to participate in the Bahrain half Ironman race in December of that year. Johnny was soon given the nickname "the lion" because of his strength and aptitude for swimming. When he joined us, he was quite stocky, but months of training would change his body dramatically. He is a good example of the positive impact that sport and a healthy lifestyle can have in a relatively short period of time.

From Thailand...

In July 2015, I went to a triathlon training camp in Thailand. I had been to Thailand before, but wanted to take the opportunity to visit some more countries and so after the training I travelled to Laos and Myanmar, countries 89 and 90 on my bucket list. Training in the summer in Qatar is virtually impossible due to the climate, and I wanted to escape the oven that most of the Arab Peninsula is in July and August.

In Thailand I trained intensively and mostly with athletes who were much better than I was, some of them even professionals. Rather than frustrating me, they inspired me. I like to be with people whose performance is better than mine, as they are the ones you can learn from. I have found that managers who dare to do the same – surround themselves with people who are smarter or better than they are themselves – perform better than "mainstream" managers who only produce "yes-men." A friend of mine described the latter as the "matroesjka" or "babuchka" syndrome. Everybody knows the small, wooden and very colourful traditional Russian dolls which can be taken off, after which a new doll appears, etcetera. However, the dolls get smaller and smaller, the more of them you remove. It is the same with managers who fear staff who might outperform them: you only produce employees or colleagues smaller than yourself, which neither benefits the company nor yourself.

On one of the last days of the camp, we had to run up a very steep hill. I was proud to be one of the first to reach the top, well before some of the "pro's" or "semi-pro's." However, the biking part was a different story. I became haunted again by my fear, with its roots in my childhood in Doha.

I was impressed by the facilities in Thailand. Obviously, Qatar has very good ones as well. However, it was the first time I had encountered facilities which were open to everyone, combined with a good hotel and healthy food. Ever since then, I have thought about bringing this concept to Qatar. Although the climate in my home country is more challenging than in Thailand during summer, it could be perfect for heat training.

It was in Thailand that I first heard about the South African Ironman race. A South African girl who was an extremely good swimmer enlightened me. She had participated in five Ironman races, including the one in South Africa. According to her, it was one of the most enchanting but also most difficult races in the world.

Execution (2015-2016)

- January 2015: started to practice triathlon
- February 2015: finished Aspire triathlon sprint (500 m swim, 20 km biking and 5 km run)
- March 2015: joined Doha Tri Club
- April 2015: finished Pearl triathlon Olympic distance (1.5 km swim, 40 km biking and 10 km run)
- July 2015: sport triathlon camp in Thailand; swim coach to improve swim technique
- December 2015: finished Bahrain half Ironman (1.9 km swim, 90 km biking and 20 km run); registered for full Ironman South Africa (10 April 2016); bought time trial (TT) road bike
- January 2016: finished Dubai half Ironman (1.9 km swim, 90 km biking and 20 km run); hired renowned international triathlon/Ironman coach
- March 2016: finished Abu Dhabi ITU world championship triathlon Olympic distance (1.5 km swim, 40 km biking and 10 km run); in the top 5 of GCC locals (i.e. locals from Gulf countries) in the age group 40-44; upgraded bike with disc wheel

… to Bahrain…

The next stop after the training camp in Thailand was the Bahrain half Ironman. Bahrain is a small and lovely island state, connected to the Arabian Peninsula by a bridge. It has quite an open atmosphere and is famed for its numerous palm trees.

"The rabbit" and I travelled together in a car packed with our gear. To reach Bahrain, first we had to travel from Qatar to Saudi Arabia. There has been talk of a bridge between Qatar and Bahrain for quite some time, but so far this is a dream, at least for some, that has not yet materialised.

December is one of the most pleasant months in the Gulf region, in terms of the weather. However, in early December 2015, Bahrain was plagued by blustery wind, which soon developed into a storm. When I saw the sea on the day before the race, fear struck my heart. The day before, we practiced in the restless waves, which made my heart sink even more, as the storm would likely swell in the hours to come, reaching its height shortly before the race was supposed to start. I hardly slept that night, feeling very anxious about what was to come. When Ebrahim and I drove to the start very early in the morning, the organisers announced that the swim would be cancelled due to the weather conditions. I didn't feel any relief. On the contrary, I was actually quite disappointed. I was participating in a very long duathlon, so to speak, and not a triathlon.

Nevertheless, the Bahrain half Ironman was a great experience, not only because it was my first Ironman race, but also because of the valuable lessons I learned from it.

First, as mentioned, I didn't sleep well the night before. Being a top athlete involves not only discipline and training, but also recovery and – a very basic need – sleep, preferably at regular hours. Having a bad night before a race is definitely not helpful.

Second, I forgot to bring the right straw for my water container for the bike and only noticed this early in the morning, a couple of hours before the start. Literally minutes before the race commenced, I was still trying to purchase a new straw to fit my water container at one of the "tri" shops typically found in the many pavilions of the racing ground. I bought a new container and used its straw, which I adjusted provisionally to fit my own container. Predictably, when I was biking I lost it, making it very difficult to drink. When I arrived home in Doha, I found the missing straw. What's the lesson here? It's all about preparation. Check your gear, if necessary two or three times and well in advance, to ensure nothing is missing. Running around the race site to get a new straw shortly before the race started was a stressful experience and not conducive to concentration.

Third, another mistake I made was not drinking enough. I did not stop at the provisioning stations as I should have done. As a result, I suffered from severe muscle ache during and after the run and nearly became dehydrated. When running, it is very important to remain adequately hydrated. It is essential either to stop at the so-called fuelling stations or to learn to drink while running. If one gets dehydrated, "the game is over," even if you are in great shape.

... to Dubai and Abu Dhabi

As we had not been able to compete in – at least from my perspective – the most challenging discipline of the Ironman race, the swim, we decided to register for the half Ironman race in Dubai due to take place in January 2016. It was Johnny, "the lion," who convinced me to do so. Initially, I hesitated when he called me. I had already registered for the Abu Dhabi triathlon in

March and felt that to be sufficient. "Come on," he said, "let's do it: the Dubai half Ironman will take place in only a month and we are in good shape after training for the half Ironman race in Bahrain." So I followed his advice.

The composition of our threesome was about to change, however. First, "the lion" decided to drop out of preparations for the Dubai half Ironman race, for very understandable personal reasons. His place was filled by Syafei, a Malaysian living in Qatar. I had noticed him before, during the triathlon at the Pearl, as he was very fast in all disciplines. He also participated in the Bahrain half Ironman race. Syafei is a small and modest man. He is the proud father of five children and has a challenging job as well. As Ebrahim was travelling a lot in this period, I trained a great deal with Syafei.

Syafei was the one who convinced me to register for the Ironman race in South Africa, which I did in January 2016. He had planned to participate there and, observing my skills, was of the view that I should register too. At first I thought he was out of his mind. Participating in a full Ironman race in April, with only one half Ironman behind me, seemed complete madness. According to the experts, one should have completed at least two half Ironman races and preferably more before entering a full Ironman race. Moreover, the South African Championship is regarded as one of the most difficult competitions. I had planned to enter a full Ironman race late in 2016, and not such a tough one. Nevertheless, his encouragement prompted me to consider it and after consulting some close friends I made up my mind to follow his advice, but I didn't communicate this to anyone and registered for it just a week before the Dubai half Ironman.

My brother and his kids accompanied me to Dubai. So far, I had not really involved my family in what I was doing. My wife knew, of course, and so did some good friends. I had also told my brother and sister and some other relatives. But apart from my wife and some friends, most of those I had told did not really understand and did not - yet - appreciate the importance of it all to me. My mother and father would only realise what I had achieved after the South African Championship. I had not involved them because they would only worry. Having said this, it was heart-warming to see how my brother supported me during the race. I am almost ten years younger than he is and very much perceived to be the younger brother. But there have not been many moments I have seen my brother so proud as during the Dubai half Ironman race, cheering and taking pictures. He was also a great help organising support from relevant organisations in the run-up to the South African Championship.

Looking back, I can see that it would have been better to involve more people in my journey. I am a pretty modest person. It is part of my personality, education and culture. My parents always taught us not to brag, as there are many people who are not as blessed as we have been. So declaring from the rooftops that I was training to become an Ironman was not in my nature. What if I did not succeed? Now I realise that involving others in achieving your dreams in life can help. Not only in terms of support, but also as a big stick to keep you on track. By sharing your objectives, you create commitment to your targets in life.

Involving my family led me to find another treasure. My sister's son became infected by his uncle's madness. He joined me many times in my training and I supported him as he learned to swim, bike and run. At the end of April 2016, he participated in a youth triathlon. We inspired each other. Since my wife and I don't have any children, bonding with my nephew created a whole new dimension. Being an Ironman runs in our family and

I sincerely hope my nephew will follow in his uncle's footsteps, if not by completing a full Ironman, at least by developing a passion for sport. As we all have to make our life journeys, some easy and some difficult, I hope that some of the lessons of being an Ironman will be of use to him as he finds his way through life.

"History repeats itself," it is often said. This indeed appeared to be the case on the eve of the Dubai half Ironman in January 2016. A storm had struck the Emirates, just like in Bahrain a month before, and the odds were that the swim would again be cancelled. The wind was even stronger than it had been then. A feeling of bitter disappointment swept over me, as I eyed the waves of the Gulf with fear and awe. When I had swum in the open sea that day, I had really struggled, so I couldn't imagine how I could possibly swim 1.9 kilometres in these conditions. The current was very strong and it was almost impossible to reach the shore. This time the organisers decided to shorten the swim to 600 metres and to move it from the open sea to Dubai's Marina. It would be followed by a 1 kilometre run to the transition area, where the bike race would start. The organisers appeared to be more in control than in Bahrain, having anticipated poor weather conditions. At least I could now participate in a half Ironman race including its first discipline, albeit only one third of the distance of the official half Ironman swim. Frankly, I was quite relieved I did not have to swim in the open sea, dragged and tossed by restless waves and a strong current.

The strong wind would nevertheless be a spoilsport. The bike course was mostly outside the city centre, in the sandy plains surrounding Dubai which are popular among tourists. As a result of the wind, this part of the race turned out to be one of the toughest I have ever done, especially the last 45 kilometres. The storm almost blew us off our bikes – and actually some athletes did fall off – and I breathed in more sand than oxygen that day. I even lost some parts of my bike because of the strong wind. As a result, I fared worse in the biking than in the Bahrain half Ironman (see the table below). I did improve on the run, though, having learned from Bahrain that I should drink enough during the race. In retrospect, I am still happy with my participation and results. I had been able to participate in the swim and it was excellent practice for the "real thing," the South African Championship in April.

Performance half Ironman:

	Dec 15 (Bahrain)	Jan 16 (Dubai)
Swimming	--	19:05
Biking	2:50:54	3:06:18
Running	2:02:49	1:55:52
Total	**4:56:57**	**5:28:02**

The last stop before my trip to South Africa would be the ITU World Championship in Abu Dhabi, in March 2016. It would be the second time I would participate in the so-called Olympic distance triathlon. This time, some good friends were there to cheer me on. The conditions in Abu Dhabi were great and I was in excellent shape. I was also extremely happy with the results (see the table below). In less than a year since I had first participated in an Olympic distance triathlon, I had improved 13 minutes on the swim, almost 30% better! On the bike, I had gained 16 minutes, an improvement of almost 20%. As for the run, I was 14 minutes faster than I had been at "The Pearl," an improvement of almost 25%. In total I was 40 minutes faster than at "The Pearl." When I told my coach, Joseph, whom I had hired to help me prepare for the Ironman race, he was delighted. The progress I had made in one year was astonishing, at least in his book. I was among the top five participants from the Gulf region in my age group in that particular race. Only a few minutes separated me from the podium.

Performance triathlon (Olympic distance)

	April 15 ("Pearl")	March 16 (Abu Dhabi)
Swimming	48:00	35:00
Biking	1:32:00	1:16:00
Running	1:02:00	48:00
Total	**3:26:00**	**2:46:00**

Lessons learned

My performance had improved substantially during 2015 and early 2016. I have already alluded to progress in the Olympic distance triathlon. As regards the sprint distance, I was more than 20 minutes faster, comparing January 2015 and April 2016, with notable progression in swimming and biking (see the table below).

Performance triathlon (sprint distance)

	Jan 15	Nov 15	Apr 16
Swimming	16:50	13:26	13:10
Biking	51:50	43:47	37:57
Running	26:17	24:00	23:14
Total	**1:38:40**	**1:24:38**	**1:17:45**

There are five reasons why my performance improved so markedly over time.

First, I was committed and disciplined. The latter sounds easier than it is. There had been many setbacks and the road was very long. What kept me on it was mainly positive thinking: the glass is always half full, not half empty. And always try to be in control. Don't let yourself be distracted or influenced by the surroundings or the scenery as you make the journey. If you do, you become cornered and are liable to surrender. This is true for the Ironman race and for every road we travel in life.

Second, I learned that training for an Ironman race is not only about endurance. It is also important to develop strength and speed. I was helped by training with "the rabbit" and "the lion" and receiving advice from other athletes, such as Bryan, an English Ironman athlete whom I met during the triathlon at the Pearl. A swim coach at the Doha TriClub helped me improve my techniques. After I decided to register for the South African Ironman race, I realised the need for professional support and hired a professional coach, Joseph, to train me in all disciplines. He had been an Ironman athlete himself and had been training Ebrahim for a while. Also in that period, the national Olympic Swimming Federation provided us with a coach to improve our techniques for swimming in open water.

Third, I realised the importance of nutrition. No-one will ever succeed in becoming an Ironman without good nutritional advice and practice. I learned the importance of eating a lot of protein, found in abundance in fruit and vegetables. The intake of carbohydrates ("carbs") is important as well, but it should mainly be done shortly before or after the race, just as it is important to increase one's intake of salt before the race, to prevent dehydration. I learned that plain water will take your legs further. Forget about energy drinks or gels, especially when training. You don't need them, only during races. They are expensive and mostly just benefit shareholders of the companies producing them. I also learned to drink during training or a race. It requires some practice but is crucial.

Fourth, you can only deliver a top performance when you have sufficient recovery: massages, rest and most importantly, just plain sleep. The situation at work was not always easy, especially after the spring of 2015. But the advantage was that I had time to train. In the months before the Ironman race, we often trained 20 hours a week. Ebrahim confessed to me that sometimes he had to take a nap at work, given our strenuous training schedule. Because of the climate, we mostly trained very early in the morning, which meant getting up shortly after the early morning prayers, at about 3.30am in Summer and 4.30am in Winter. In early 2016, we began training twice a day, most days of the week, including covering long distances at the weekend. When Joseph sent us the weekly training schedule, I hardly dared open my email. Once I could not sleep, having seen what he had planned for us.

So recovery is a key success factor for every Ironman athlete or anyone who is required to perform at the highest level. It is quite common for businessmen or government officials to work 60 to 80 hours a week, in particular in the western world. It is part of a culture of "winning" and "performing," and nobody wants to leave the office before the boss has gone home. But this road is a dead end, since a top performance can only be delivered by leading a balanced life and having sufficient recovery time. It is not without reason that the number of young professionals suffering from "burn-out," or worse, has increased rapidly.

Finally, and on a more personal level, I gradually mastered

some of my fears. Swimming was never my favourite triathlon discipline and I struggled a lot. Partly this was caused by a lack of technical skills. I only learned in early 2016 that my techniques had so far not been good. I also feared the water. As a kid, I once had a disturbing experience while swimming with my friends in the sea near Dukhan, off the north-western coast of the country. Strong currents prevented me from swimming back to shore and I feared I was about to drown. Eventually I felt the ground under my feet again, but the experience haunted me for a long time. Despite my efforts, swimming would be the most challenging part of the South African Championship. Also, on the bike I was not always steady, especially when going fast downhill. I gradually mastered this as well, learning the importance of a good 'cadence'.

However, 'safety first' would remain my motto. I never endangered my life or health, as some others might have done. My background as an engineer was also of great value. Anybody who works in the oil and gas industry knows that health and security always come first.

Does this mean that I didn't make any mistakes in this period? Luckily I did. In the autumn, while I was strengthening the muscles in my back at home, I felt, and actually heard, something snapping in my left latisissimus dorsi. The next day I had a local race planned. Instead of listening to my body and cancelling the race, I participated, inflicting a very painful muscle injury upon myself. For many days I could hardly walk and I seriously feared I would not be able to participate in the Bahrain half Ironman race. It was then only three weeks before the race. I did recover in time. However, this experience again underlined the importance of 'safety first'.

From concept, incubation and acceleration to deployment and full production

Ironman athletes take different roads to reach the same objective. Following the steps of "strategy and planning", then "execution", suited me and my personality well. It is how I was taught to proceed in projects in the oil and gas industry. Indeed, technological development and innovation are marked by three stages.

It all starts with an idea, or concept. For me this was the Ironman TV coverage in 1988.

The second stage entails experimenting, building prototypes and testing them in a controlled environment. This is called "sandboxing" or the "incubator phase." An important feature of this phase is that things can go wrong. Actually, they should go wrong. This is when the prototype is improved, and one learns from setbacks and mistakes. It is also the most critical phase of the process. Many innovations go wrong in the incubation period. My incubation stage was the period from 1988 until 2014.

The final stage is the "acceleration phase." This phase is typically much shorter, its aim being to test and prepare for the full production or commercialisation of an innovation. It is characterised by an intensive use of resources – like my training in 2015 and 2016 – and the stakes have become pretty high. The innovation can still be put on a shelf, but often at great cost for investors or the company or organisation concerned. My "acceleration phase" started in early 2015, leading me to "full production," the start of the Ironman race in April 2016.

"All roads lead to Rome." This is true for any Ironman journey. If Ebrahim were to write a book about his experiences, it would be a different one. Still, there is always a phase of preparation and planning involved. And what is true for any successful innovation is also true for the journey to become an Ironman – you will fail without it.

Chapter 3

Swimming

I dive with long strokes,
In a triple adventure,
That started with a dream.
Competing against myself,
Breathing – left and right,
Like a knife cutting the billow,
Straight to my purpose in life.

The start

When I woke up on Saturday, 10th April 2016, the sun had not yet risen. It was four o'clock in the morning. From the window of our hotel suite, I could see the site where, in about three hours, the African Championship of the Ironman would start. My wife and I had only recently moved to this hotel. When we arrived in South Africa, we first stayed a couple of days in Cape Town before continuing our journey towards Port Elizabeth and my wife got a serious cold. My coach advised me to take two rooms to avoid being infected myself. As we were not able to book another room in the first hotel, we moved to a two-bedroom suite in a different one, which happened to overlook the start and finish of the Ironman race and the Indian Ocean. I felt very sorry for my wife, but I could not take the risk of catching a cold myself, so close before "D-Day". As always, she fully understood. Actually, I was not feeling well myself. I had started to develop serious stomach problems after our arrival in South Africa. I should probably not have eaten that salad… I really had felt miserable during the first days in Cape Town and had not been sleeping very well either. I was really worried that I would have to cancel just as I was about to reach the end of my journey. Luckily, I recovered shortly before we moved to Port Elizabeth, but my body did not feel as if it were in top condition.

As always in life, every disadvantage has its advantage. The new hotel was in a much better location than the previous one. My wife would probably have to spend more than 12 hours here, killing time while I was competing in the race, so staying opposite the site was pretty convenient.

For this final part of my Ironman journey, I was accompanied by my wife. We had planned to go on holiday after the race to Namibia and Botswana, another two countries to add to my list. But more important than a holiday, I felt she should witness the outcome of all my efforts in the last couple of years. It was a reward for her too, as she had given me unswerving support. I can assure you, training for an Ironman race is not necessarily good for a marriage. It demands endurance and the same holds true for the wife or husband of an Ironman athlete.

We had arrived in Port Elizabeth a couple of days before "racing day." It is always good to arrive at least two days before the start of a race, especially when you are not familiar with the location. First, to acclimatise, especially when a change of time zone is involved. If there is a big time difference, arriving two days in advance will not be enough. Second, it is important to check the racecourse in advance. Ideally, you should swim or bike a few laps, assessing the conditions and testing the bike.

Finally, there are quite a lot of administrative and practical issues which need to be taken care of, like registering yourself and putting your gear in place.

The areas where triathletes change from one discipline to the other are called transition zones. The first transition area, usually labelled T1, is where you swap your wet suit and swimming gear for your bike, which is waiting for you, like an obedient horse for his master. You can also put your helmet and other gear needed for the bike race in a blue plastic bag and deliver it to the organisers in advance, so it is waiting for you when you arrive in the transition area after the swim. Stuff you don't need, after the swim, you can put in the bag. The second transition (T2) denotes the area where you return your bike and change for the final discipline of the triathlon, the run. The same procedure applies, the blue bag now being replaced by a red one, with your running gear in it, into which you can drop redundant items after the bike race.

Port Elizabeth

Port Elizabeth is one of the major cities in South Africa; Nelson Mandela Bay, where it is situated, is named after South Africa's first post-apartheid president, and has approximately 1.3 million inhabitants. The city, also called "The Bay," is located on the Indian Ocean, about 800 kilometres east of Cape Town. It is also nicknamed "The Friendly City" or "The Windy City," referring to the strong winds that can plague it. By and large, the climate is mild, with average high temperatures in the summer (January) of around 25C and 9C in winter (July). Port Elizabeth was one of the South African cities which hosted the 2010 FIFA football World Championship, of which the Nelson Mandela Bay Stadium is a remnant. The stadium is nowadays used by the Eastern Province Rugby Union.

When we arrived in Port Elizabeth and I caught sight of the Indian Ocean, I wondered whether I had suffered a fit of insanity when I agreed to register for the African Championship. The ghosts of the sea seemed to have been haunting me ever since the Bahrain half Ironman race. Why could I not for once have the chance to swim in open water that was tranquil? Maybe I should have known better when I read the nickname of Port Elizabeth - "The Windy City." Vast waves thundered and rolled across the Indian Ocean. When I went out for a trial swim on the day before the race, the water was cold and the currents were very strong. To make things worse, I was told that not only triathletes but also sharks loved to circle in Port Elizabeth's coastal waters. Less than a year ago, the Australian surfing star Mick Fanning had barely survived a shark attack during a surfing match at Jeffreys Bay, east of Port Elizabeth. Luckily I had not yet seen the blockbuster movie "The Shallows," a modern version of "Jaws" released in the summer of 2016, triggering our worst subconscious nightmares about "the great white." I was very happy my mother did not know what I was about to do. Frankly, I didn't want to know myself either. Since we had moved to our new hotel, I had been watching the ocean from the balcony of our room, trying to assess whether the waves were getting bigger or if the sea was becoming calmer. Unfortunately, it continued to roar relentlessly.

I admit that I am sometimes a "last minute man." When I travel, I like to use my time as efficiently as possible and I am rarely the first to appear at the airport gate. It sometimes unnerves the people I travel with. "I like suspense," I jokingly tell my travel companions as they are eying their watches, afraid of missing a flight. Also on this particular morning, I had to hurry to get to the starting point on time, despite the fact that I could see it from the window of my hotel room. I should really have got out of bed earlier. Since I was late, I had no time for a proper warm-up, a necessity when starting the Ironman race, especially in the early morning when your muscles are still lethargic from sleep.

Arriving at the starting point, I felt shivers down my spine, in the presence of the other 1,856 athletes, both professionals and amateurs. The sight was spectacular. Men and women with swimming caps on, in different colours according to their age group, were waiting for the rolling start of the swim. The images burned into my mind of the TV coverage of the first Ironman race I had seen back in 1988, returned.

A rolling start means that athletes do not start at the same time, but in small groups, in this case 10 swimmers every 5 seconds. The rolling start was introduced to avoid swimmers literally falling over each other and to prevent them from kicking each other instead of the water. Swimmers were requested to organise themselves into four groups: those who would swim 3.8

kilometres in less than one hour; or between one hour and one hour and a half; or one and a half and two hours and finally, the swimmers estimating they would need more than two hours for the swim. A cut-off time was announced: any swimmer taking more than two hours and 20 minutes to reach the first transition would be disqualified.

With "the lion" about to return to his home country, it would be "the rabbit" and "the turtle," together with their Malaysian friend, finishing this last part of the journey. We were like Alexandre Dumas's "the three musketeers," Aramis, Athos and Porthos, their famous battle cry being "all for one, and one for all." Ebrahim, "the rabbit," had joined us in Cape Town and Port Elizabeth. We had a lovely dinner together in Cape Town before my stomach started to protest. When we arrived at the starting point, he talked me into joining the second fastest group, which turned out to be a big mistake. Ebrahim, who is 15 years younger than I am, is a great friend and an amazing and very promising athlete and filled with ambition and energy. Being the "turtle," I should have known better, but the desire to be at his side won over rational considerations, so I joined him in this group of swimmers.

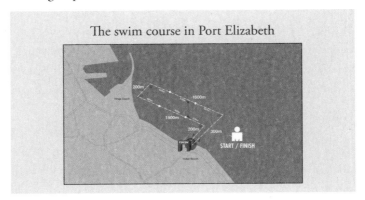

The swim course in Port Elizabeth

The abyss

At 6.30am the first swimmers, the professionals, entered the water. We gradually moved forward in the direction of the start. Then it was our turn. My coach Joseph had advised me to enter the water with force, at least for the first 200 metres. This would put you into racing mood, help you to master the surf, stay warm and prevent you from being paralysed by the cold water or choked by the waves, and get you to the first buoy with vigour. I ran across the beach towards the water of the Indian Ocean. The sun had just risen, giving the water a glare. My feet touched the water. When my feet could no longer carry me, I started to swim.

I suddenly felt entangled by the legs and arms of other athletes, and since I had opted, too ambitiously, for the second time group, swimmers faster than me were pressing on me from behind. I couldn't stretch out my arms or legs anymore, stuck in a tangle of body parts. I felt as if I was inside a washing machine or like spaghetti about to be boiled for a nice Italian dinner. Besides starting in the wrong time group, I had made another mistake: I had moved myself into the middle of the group of swimmers. As a result, I couldn't move forwards, backwards or sideways, even if I wanted to. But these were not the only sensations I had. The strong current and massive waves caught me off guard. The water was lifting and pushing me wherever it wanted to. I felt like a ship about to be wrecked, no longer in control.

It was the worst moment of the whole race. Actually, the worst moment of my whole journey. I was completely panic-stricken and no longer able to move. I could hardly keep myself afloat. And to make matters worse, I became aware of a cramp in my left calf and hamstring. "Game over," I thought. I was about to quit, was metaphorically speaking a matter of inches away from doing so and swimming back to shore. I was completely overwhelmed by my fears.

Then the faces of the people who had been supporting me throughout my journey appeared in my mind. They were watching me, via the internet or other means, all over the world. They were anxious and full of hope that today I would complete my journey. I could hear their cheers, their voices, feel their arms embracing me or their mouths kissing me; see their eyes, full of sympathy, kindness and love. It was at that moment that I decided to continue. I would not disappoint them. And, more importantly, I would not disappoint myself either.

I calmed down and took two very important decisions as I regained control. First, I moved as fast as I could to the side of the group of swimmers. This would prevent me from colliding with them all the time. In fact, this was exactly what Joseph, my coach, had advised me to do in the first place. Then I remembered the advice given to me by a close friend some two weeks before. He knew I was dreading the swim, just as some people dread going to the dentist. He had advised me not to fight the waves, but to bond with them. "They are your friends," he said, "not your enemies." The best helmsmen stand on shore, and my friend is not a good swimmer himself. Nevertheless, he was right. I literally went with the flow. Or, as my friend had advised me, "do not try to cut the waves as a knife cuts butter, but let the waves carry you." Finally and perhaps most importantly, I was able to recharge by starting to think positively. I had done this before, so why falter now? The glass is not half empty, it is half full.

The swim: challenges, mistakes and solutions

Challenges	Mistakes	Solutions
• cold water, strong currents and massive waves • shock/panic after first 200 metres • faster swimmers pressing from behind • stuck in middle of swimmers' group • muscle cramp • overwhelmed by worries; about to quit	• got up too late; no time for warm-up before start • joined inappropriate time group at rolling start • swimming in the centre of the swimmers' group	• positive thinking • be in control • move to the edge of the swimmers' group • bond with the waves

So I slowly started to swim in the Indian Ocean again: 200 metres, 300 metres… and gradually regained my confidence. The serious cramp in my left calf and hamstring wore off when I began swimming again. I re-took control of my mind. After the long hours of training I had been enduring, I knew I was physically able to finish the race, and in a matter of minutes, my mood changed completely. From being in sheer panic, I now started to enjoy swimming in the ocean.

Water world

The swim course first brought us 300 metres out from the

coast, followed by a left turn and a swim of 1600 metres until the next turn. Then we had to swim back to the coastline for another 200 metres and turn, followed by another 1500 metres of swimming, before reaching the final turn to the right towards the end. So the currents and direction of the waves changed all the time, but this is where my experience in swimming in open water came in. I had been doing so back home twice a week for a month and a half before the Ironman race. When I swam out, the waves were approaching me. They tilted me from the right during the first long haul, and to the left during the second one. After the second turn, when we were swimming back to the coast again, and shortly before the finish, the waves came from behind. Actually, the latter was a rather tedious experience as it felt like I was pulled back into the sea after every wave, unlike the waves that approached me from the side, which did not really bother me.

When I swim, I usually tilt my head slightly to the right to breathe. During the first long haul, after the first turn, I glimpsed the vastness of the Indian Ocean. As I had moved to the edge of the pack of swimmers, there was hardly anyone else in sight. It was an amazing feeling, as if I was a large ship sailing the ocean. At the same time I had to keep my course and watch the buoys in the water. This was not easy, as they sometimes vanished because of the waves. Still, I managed to keep sight of them. When I turned towards the city, I had the pleasure of seeing the buildings of Port Elizabeth come into view. It almost felt as if I was running towards the shore.

This all sounds very romantic, but it should be noted that an Ironman race, especially the swim, requires a lot of organisation and caretaking, the main objective being to ensure the safety of the athletes. Little barges and kayaks surrounded us, with staff standing by to assist if anything should go wrong. There were, deliberately, no motorised boats tracking the swimmers, as they might cause unnatural waves or air pollution. Halfway across the course was a huge platform in the sea, almost a hospital, from which medical assistance or help could be provided.

The world on water is totally different from the world on land. The scene on this early morning of 10th April 2016 was like something from the movie Waterworld, featuring Kevin Costner. It was a motley of swimmers, with different coloured swimming caps, arms and legs causing the water to break, surfers cheering the swimmers in the water, and a collection of boats tracking the swimmers like a hen guarding its chicks. The big crowd who had come to Port Elizabeth to watch the Ironman race was on the shore. Their role had been limited so far, as they could hardly grasp what was going on in the water. They would really come into their own during the bike course and the marathon.

As I do for any long race, I had divided the course into smaller segments, nine this time, from buoy to buoy, to make it seem shorter. This helped me to be focused and in control. It might be difficult to imagine, but one does a lot of thinking during an Ironman race. All kinds of thoughts crossed my mind, about projects I had been working on, my family and friends, the many countries I had visited, favourite films or TV shows, sport, and also thoughts about people who were not my close friends. These thoughts can be quite strange, like some dreams we have, and I will not entrust them to the pages of this book. Having a blank mind is not helpful during an Ironman race. Thoughts keep you focused and help you maintain your cadence. This is especially important on the bike and during the marathon.

Results of the swim

Distance	Time	Pace
3.8 km	1:51:52	2:56/100m

When I looked at my watch, approximately halfway, I realised I would reach the finish well within the cut-off time if I continued at the current pace. I felt more relaxed and was even able to increase my pace during the last 1 kilometre. I would finish in one hour and 50 minutes approximately, about half an hour before cut-off time. I could have been about 15 minutes faster if I had not had the crisis at the beginning.

Five years ago I had practiced a 5 kilometre swim. It took me five hours to finish it. An Ironman race requires you to finish a course of slightly less than 4 kilometres in 2 hours and 20 minutes maximum. As you can imagine, a lot of training and discipline was required to get me here from that starting point.

How did my friends fare? "The rabbit" finished the swim in 1 hour and 22 minutes, 67th in his age group. If I had not lost 15 minutes at the beginning, we would have been pretty close. Syafei from Malaysia finished in 1 hour and 40 minutes, 297th in his age group. If I had not had my crisis, I might even have been faster than him.

Conquering the sea

When my feet touched the beach of Port Elizabeth again, I was ecstatically happy. I had finished one of the most challenging Ironman swim courses, known for its treacherous currents and massive waves. I had also finished the discipline that was my least favourite and which took me out of my comfort zone. I had really dreaded it. As I undertook it, there was no Qatari Michael Phelps or Pieter van den Hoogenband to take as my example.

Paulo Coelho wrote in "The Alchemist:" "Tell your heart that the fear of suffering is worse than the suffering itself. And that no heart has ever suffered when it goes in search of its dreams, because every second of the search is a second's encounter with God and with eternity." To master your fears, you have to face them and get out of your comfort zone. Only then will you develop and grow. Without consciously planning it, I was facing my fears head on. I had beaten the sea ghosts of Bahrain and Dubai that had been haunting me, as well as traumatic memories of nearly drowning as a teenager, and as a result I later entered the open water, in early May 2016 in Doha, with a completely different feeling. Swimming is still the most challenging discipline for me, but I am no longer afraid of the open water. Quite the contrary.

Maybe this was the moment I truly became an Ironman. I did not let my fears and worries cripple me. I decided to conquer them by staying positive, putting into practice the advice of my coach and friend, and realising that I was not only doing this for myself, but also for those who had offered me their unconditional support throughout my journey.

Chapter 4

Biking

Then I rise,
Focused in transition,
Shoes, helmet and spanning the pedals,
Of my steel steed.
My muscles tense,
Finding ryhthm and pace,
Onto the last part of the race.

Rising from the water

When I left the Indian Ocean to move to the first transition, I was physically in good shape. I even ran out of the water onto the beach. In the photos taken in that moment, my face looks strong. I wanted to make up the time I had lost during the swim. However, mentally I was not in very good shape, despite the fact that I felt triumphant, having finished what was for me the most difficult discipline of the triathlon. For whatever reason – maybe it was being almost two hours in the water - I had lost focus and my mind was empty. It is certainly a peculiar feeling to be on land again after the sea. Gravity makes your limbs feel heavy at first. I had also started to feel dizzy and my stomach had begun to ache.

The transition to the bike means turning yourself from a fish-like creature into a mammal. I freed myself from the upper part of my wet suit before landing on shore. While I ran to the transition area, I removed my swimming cap and goggles and swapped them for my helmet, sunglasses and socks which were waiting for me in the blue bag. I then moved to the tent containing the bikes. As I entered, I noticed that athletes had already mounted about 75 per cent of the bikes, while 25 per cent of the steel steeds still patiently waited for their owners who were struggling in the water. Staff helped me remove the lower part of the wet suit. Obviously, you wear your biking and running outfit underneath the wet suit. I put on my socks, helmet and glasses and jumped on the bike. My shoes were already attached to the pedals.

Attaching the shoes to the bike beforehand turned out to be a bad idea. When every second matters, in a shorter sprint or Olympic distance triathlon, and when one is less disoriented, having not spent that long in the water, it is the appropriate thing to do. But after almost two hours in the sea, you run the risk of falling off your bike as you jump onto it and get into your shoes. And this is what happened. As I left the transition area, I lost my balance and fell, swerving to the right and injuring my right knee, which started to bleed heavily. So the transition from the swim to the bike took me almost seven and a half minutes. If I had just packed my shoes in the bag and put them on before mounting the bike, I would not have fallen off and had such a long transition.

The solitude of a bike

So I began the 180.2 kilometre bike course feeling unfocused and dizzy, with an upset stomach and an injured knee. Still, riding the first kilometres was soothing, using different muscles and being in a different position than horizontal in the water. Human beings are not made to live in the sea. The temperature was also still comfortable at that time of the day – it was mid-morning – and the light breeze dried and cooled my body.

The bike course is hailed as one of the most beautiful of the Ironman races worldwide, and I would not dare to challenge this assertion. Being a contender did not allow me to enjoy it as much as if I had been a plain tourist. Still, I could enjoy the beauty of the scenery and the stunning view of the Indian Ocean.

The course consisted of two loops of 90 kilometres, with a grand view of the Indian Ocean during most of the ride. It was hilly, including two elevations of 685 and 681 metres respectively. After about 20 kilometres, we encountered a steep 100 metre hill (Schoenmakerskop), followed by a gradual decline to the turning point. Then it went gradually uphill again, followed by a steep decline back to the beach. When you think you have achieved your target, with the end of the Ironman race in sight, you realise you have to repeat the loop. This was probably one of the most difficult moments in the race.

The bike course

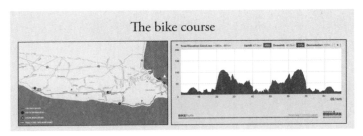

As with the swim, I had subdivided the course into smaller trajectories, to make it less daunting. My thoughts were not on the long haul I had to bike, but on that particular segment. It was like reading a book, chapter after chapter.

Lessons learned

The major issue during the bike ride was nutrition. When biking, nutrition is key, and one should think it through well in advance. Biking is usually the longest of the three Ironman disciplines. I spent almost two hours in the water, more than seven hours on the bike and just over five hours running. To put things in perspective, the biking took about as long as a journey by plane from Doha to London. Obviously, the circumstances are quite different when you are sitting in a nice chair, watching a film and receiving your food and drinks at regular intervals (I tell this to people a lot, nowadays, who complain about having to fly economy class on a long-haul flight!). In addition, one has already consumed a lot of energy while swimming and there is no opportunity to replace this while in the water. So it is of paramount importance to refuel as soon as possible when on the bike. Without nutrition and water, it will soon be "game over," even if one is physically in great shape. Measuring your nutrition and water intake well involves meticulous planning. And like everything in life, a job well conceived is a job half done.

I had two bottles of fluid nutrition and one bottle of water. Obviously, one needs to drink more, but there are several "refuelling stations" along the course. My coach had told me to put the bottle with a high concentration of carbs (carbohydrates) in the container at the front of the bike between my legs and the other bottle, containing a lower concentration of carbs, at the back. His advice was to start drinking from the back bottle and use it for the first hour or so. Given the condition I was in, after the backbreaking swim, I should have started drinking from the bottle in the front container. I felt myself weakening in the first three hours while I was drinking from the low carb concentration fluid, taking a sip every 20 minutes. I was gradually dehydrating, which is difficult to realise when you are biking.

I am definitely not questioning the advice of my coach. Compare it to the feeding schedule a wet nurse provides you when a baby is born: one is taught to feed the baby a specific amount of milk after a specific period of time. These schedules are based on long experience of feeding children, but they are averages. In reality, no new-born is the same. Some babies require more milk and others less. When the baby is your first-born, you stick to the schedule meticulously, afraid of making mistakes, even if the child continues to cry after a bottle. However, you gradually realise, and this is particularly true for the second or third child, that it might be appropriate to deviate from the prescribed feeding schedule, based on your own experience as a parent.

After the first 90 kilometre loop, I started to drink from the bottle in the front. The impact was immediate. I felt my energy levels increasing and was able to focus again. Still, after 90 kilometres I was physically tired, and I also felt the impact of the weather. It was past noon and the sun was directly overhead in the sky. The temperature and humidity were unusually high for the late South African summer and the wind had also increased. I should have drunk more water, as I underestimated the impact of the differences in elevation. True, I was not biking in the Alps, but we still had to reach a height of more than 100 metres four times during the course.

I made another mistake. I had purchased a rather expensive disc wheel for my bike. From experience, disc wheels provide less friction, allowing you to bike faster when you reach threshold speed of around 30 kilometres per hour. However, using a disc wheel makes the bike less flexible. I had not reckoned with the poor conditions of a large part of the course. The disc wheel became a disadvantage as the bike started to shake and I could not reach threshold speed. I had to hold the aero bar very tight to remain stable and I soon developed blisters that started to bleed. As it was my aim to finish the race safe, especially as I had already fallen off the bike and had felt so weak during the first part of the race, I decided to reduce my speed.

The bike ride: challenges, mistakes and solutions

Challenges	Mistakes	Solutions
• stomach upset • fell off bike at the start and injured right knee • dizzy after swim and subsequent lack of focus during the first 90 km loop • very warm and humid during second 90 km loop • hilly course (5 to 110 metres) • partially poor condition of the road	• shoes attached to the pedals of my bike in advance • used two water bottles with different carb concentration and started drinking from the bottle with lowest concentration first • used disc wheel, which was not appropriate for the course	• safety first; avoid falling off the bike • avoid too high speed • thinking and talking to myself to stay focused and keep awake • use higher carb concentration at the beginning of the race • avoid dehydration and becoming overheated, e.g. by pouring water over me • think positive • be in control

An important lesson of the bike race is the importance of managing time and energy effectively, including the intake of energy and water. Another lesson concerns one's overall stamina and physical and mental abilities. The fact that the course consisted of two loops of 90 kilometres did not help. After the first loop, your body tells you to stop and end this insane activity. You realise that you have to do the whole loop again, climbing the same hills, facing the wind again and coping again with the road conditions which were sometimes poor. At this moment, it is of the utmost importance to stay positive, and to achieve this it helps to stay focused. I had written the names of people on my arms, both people I care about as well as people who are not my intimate friends. From time to time, I looked at my arm. I started to think about those people and the circumstances that define them, both positively as well as negatively. I even started talking to myself. My nickname "the turtle" also helped. It was given to me because of my ability to pace myself during an endurance race and my attitude of perseverance and refusing to give in, despite the many obstacles in my way.

The crowd along the course also helped immensely, more than I had expected. In the swim, the crowd had been on the shore, barely able to see what was going on in the water. So you are really on your own, with the exception of a few windsurfers tracking you. Everybody who watches legendary bike races like the Tour de France knows the images of the public standing on the slopes of infamous mountains such as the Tourmalet or Alpe d'Huez, shouting and cheering the cyclists to the top. "Murderers," the first cyclists exclaimed when reaching the "cols" during the early days of the Tour de France, referring to the organisers of the most famous bike race in the world. Although the numbers cheering us were not comparable to those on the famous ascents of the Tour de France or Giro d'Italia, they were still impressive and their support literally gave me wings when I needed them most. For many of the supporters it was like going to a big festival. Music was playing and their good mood and high spirits affected me positively.

Results of the biking

Distance	(Split) time	Pace (km/h)	(Race) time
43 km	1:37:57	26.34	3:37:12
47 km	14:30	16.55	3:51:42
90 km	1:44:16	24.74	5:35:58
133 km	1:39:52	25.83	7:15:50
137 km	12:54	18.60	7:28:44
180 km	1:50:43	23.30	9:19:27
Total	**7:20:12**	**24.53**	**9:19:27**

Two out of three

I finished the bike course in seven hours and twenty minutes, at an average pace of almost 25 kilometres per hour. The split results (see table above) do not give any indication that I was in a weak, unfocused state for the first three hours of the race. Actually, I performed better then than during the second part of the race. The reason for this is that later, although my energy levels were up and I was more focused, fatigue had kicked in. The kilometres weighed on my muscles and bones, and I was affected by the rise in temperature and humidity. Plus, I decided not to ride at maximum speed, given the poor road conditions and stiffness of my bike because of the disc wheel. I was applying the motto of "Safety first," and I was especially careful on the descents. In relative terms, I did somewhat better than in the swim, ranking 297th in my age group. I had gained back some of the time lost in the water.

Chapter 5

The run

Both feet on the ground,
Running a distance,
Equalling Marathon to Athens.
My body hurts,
My eyes focusing on infinity,
But with an iron will,
To show what endurance can achieve.
Hungry for the finish line.

From Marathon to Port Elizabeth

It was a warm day in the late summer of the year 490 BC, probably as warm and humid as 10th April 2016, in the late summer of Port Elizabeth. The armies of Greece had just defeated the gargantuan army of the Persians. The stench on the battlefield at Marathon was breathtaking. One could still smell the sweat of the soldiers slain on the field, mixed with an odour of blood and flesh that had already started to decay under the burning sun. The Greek armies roared and proclaimed victory. Pheidippides, messenger of the Athenian army, was overjoyed when he started his journey of approximately 40 kilometres from the battlefield to his native city. He ran, the victory providing him with wings. And when he passed the city gates, he immediately made his way to the leaders of Athens, assembled together at the Acropolis. "Nikomen – we have won," he shouted. Then his heart stopped beating and he dropped down dead on the marble stairs.

The story of Pheidippides

So, when Persia was dust, all cried "To Acropolis!"
Run, Pheidippides, one race more! the meed is thy due!
"Athens is saved, thank Pan, go shout!" He flung down his shield,
Ran like fire once more: and the space 'twixt the Fennel-field,
And Athens was stubble again, a field which a fire runs through,
Till in he broke: "Rejoice, we conquer!" Like wine thro' clay,
Joy in his blood bursting his heart, he died--the bliss!
So, to this day, when friend meets friend, the word of salute,
Is still "Rejoice!"- his word which brought rejoicing indeed.
So is Pheidippides happy forever,- the noble strong man
Who could race like a god, bear the face of a god, whom a god loved so well;
He saw the land saved he had helped to save, and was suffered to tell,
Such tidings, yet never decline, but, gloriously as he began,
So to end gloriously - once to shout, thereafter be mute:
"Athens is saved!" - Pheidippides dies in the shout for his meed.

From: Robert Browning, "Pheidippides" (1870)

There was a lot of drama in 490 BC, or so the annals would have us believe. Many historians and poets have dwelled on this historical event, which is at the roots of the modern marathon. The reality was probably less heroic. To honour the ancient foundations of the Olympic Games, the marathon was introduced at the first modern Olympics which took place in Athens in 1896. The distance of this first marathon was 25 miles. In 1908 at the Olympic Games in London, it was extended to 26 miles. This was not because historians had discovered that this was the precise distance run by Pheidippides, but because this suited the British royal family. It was the distance from Windsor Castle, where the marathon began, to the finish line in front of the royal stand at the White City Stadium. Ever since, the official distance of the marathon has been 26 miles, or 42 kilometres and 195 metres.

There was also quite a lot of drama on 10th April 2016. To torture the athletes - or, positively framed, to provide them with incentive to perform - the Port Elizabeth marathon was staged along the beachfront, with the end of the Ironman race more or less constantly in sight, and the transition area – the same one for switching from swimming to biking – next to it. Athletes had to run four laps of 10.55 kilometres. After leaving the transition area, they had to head right until they reached a turning point, then run back and pass the finish line and the transition area, until a second turning point, after which they had to complete the last part of the loop, bringing them back to the finish again. At the aid station, just prior to the first turning point, we were issued with a band to tie around our wrists. This indicated how many laps were completed. And since many athletes would be running in the dark, glow sticks were also distributed. I would witness the sunset, having run approximately 20 kilometres, while the professional athletes would finish well before the darkness set in.

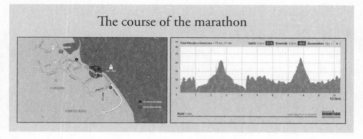

The course of the marathon

The running experience

When I approached the transition point, I speeded up, as if I had been given wings. I pushed on. The last part of the trajectory led across a number of dunes and after each turn I craved the sight of the houses of Port Elizabeth. They were like angels announcing my approach to the transition. The improved quality of the asphalt, providing some relief to my strained body, was the first sign I was nearing the end of the bike race. The road had been really poor and riding it with my disc wheel had been a torture. My energy levels were up again as I entered the outskirts of Port Elizabeth. I was engulfed by happiness when I rode into the transition area, having spent more than seven hours hunched on my bike, hands glued to the handlebars and arms stiff as a pole. I felt like an animal finally set free from its cage, able to use all its muscles and move around freely again. It was a magical feeling when my feet touched the surface of the planet again. After riding 180 kilometres, standing on the ground again is a wonderful experience.

The challenges of running are different from those of biking or swimming. First, the heartbeat is much higher when running or swimming, creating a different experience of fatigue. Second, although both biking and running primarily involve one's legs, the pressure on one's knees and feet is obviously quite different during the run. Most importantly, the marathon is about managing your energy levels. Running 42.2 kilometres is a strenuous undertaking. However, running such a distance after almost 4 kilometres swimming and 180 kilometres biking is a huge challenge. It is vital to have sufficient energy left when stepping off the bike. If not, the Ironman race will not end well, despite one's best efforts. For this reason, the back-up services constantly scrutinise the athletes, especially during the run, to detect signs of exhaustion and prevent them going from bad to worse. Runners who sway about are summarily removed from the race.

It took me a while to start the marathon after parking my bike. The transition area was large and I had to empty my bladder, despite the fact that one loses so much fluid through one's pores during a race like this. I felt fresh when I started the run. If I could maintain my starting pace, my racing time would really be good. About four hours, I thought. I was also happy that I was no longer dependent on something mechanical – a bike – to keep me going, with all the risks involved, like falling off. It was now just down to my feet and myself.

In my perception, I performed best during the first 10 kilometres of the marathon, better than any other section of the whole race. The first metres in the water had been a nightmare, as elaborated in chapter 3, and the first kilometres on the bike had been difficult. Still, when I look at my overall performance in the marathon (see the table below), my speed was fairly regular throughout the run, which is obviously good. Of course, success is not just measured by speed, but also by one's overall physical and mental condition. And I really felt good during the first 10 kilometres of the run, enjoying the attention of the crowd and a different discipline, after being stuck to a bike.

Results of the marathon

Distance	(Split) time	Pace (km/h)	(Race) time
2 km	14:03	7:01	9:39:10
5.3 km	20:54	6:20	10:00:13
7.4 km	12:18	5:51	10:12:31
10.5 km	20:45	6:41	10:33:16
12.5 km	16:06	8:03	10:49:22
15.8 km	23:48	7:12	11:13:10
17.9 km	14:18	6:48	11:27:28
21 km	23:22	7:32	11:50:50
23 km	18:10	9:05	12:09:00
26.3 km	26:46	8:06	12:35:46
28.4 km	15:07	7:11	12:50:53
31.5 km	24:33	7:55	13:15:26
33.5 km	18:15	9:07	13:33:41
36.8 km	28:26	8:36	14:02:07
38.9 km	15:41	7:28	14:17:48
42.2 km	25:30	7:43	14:43:18
Total	**5:18:02**	**7:32**	**14:43:18**

Shortly after I left the transition area and started running, I saw my friend Ebrahim. He was well ahead of me and had already run about 20 kilometres. The age difference between us accounted for this, but I was very proud of his achievement. I was running with a female athlete during the first part of the race, which helped me maintain my excellent starting pace. Unlike swimming and biking, running is social. I talked to some of the other athletes and at the end of the marathon joined up with another female athlete. We agreed that running together would help us cross the finish line.

Anyone craving solitude during the run would have been frustrated. The place was packed. Thousands of spectators stood behind the barriers, shouting, applauding and cheering at their friends or family. My wife was one of them. I started to recognize people in the audience while re-passing them during the four loops of the race, especially just before one of the turning points where the road became steeper and runners reduced their speed.

It was strictly forbidden to wear earplugs during the race to listen to your favourite music or a pre-recorded inspirational speech by your coach. In any case, it was not necessary here. There was music everywhere; the event rivalled the best pop festivals. It was like a carnival and people were even having barbecues along the course.

The athletes themselves crowded the laps, made up of two lanes with two-way traffic on them. On part of the course, there was two-way biking as well as running. Traffic wardens would have been useful! The buzz of the event created a very special atmosphere, in remarkable contrast to the 'Waterworld' experience of the swim and the solitude of the bike. This atmosphere boosted the athletes' spirits and helped to carry them over the finishing line.

However, after about an hour and a half, I started to lose focus and suffer dizzy spells. The beautiful view of the sea no longer provided comfort. Fatigue and warm weather were taking a heavy toll on my body, but the real problem was that I had started to become dehydrated.

I was saved by drinking lots of Coca-Cola at the fuelling stations along the course. It provided the necessary liquidity and kept me awake. Compared to many other people, the caffeine probably had a greater impact on my body, as I never drink coffee or sodas. I probably consumed more caffeine during the Ironman race than I had done during my entire life up to that point. Luckily, neither Cola nor caffeine are registered as doping drugs. It also helped me that I decided not to stop. I continued to run, although I saw many athletes, like my Malaysian friend and training buddy, walking from time to time. As much as possible, I tried to maintain my pace. I realised that stopping or walking might be the end of my race.

Eventually I managed to regain focus, yet after having been in the water and on the road for about 12 hours, my body started to protest. After about 25 to 30 kilometres, I started to develop serious knee problems. In order to limit the pain in my knee, I tried to maintain a high cadence by taking smaller steps. About 5 kilometres before the finish line, my body was screaming that I should stop. The ends of my nerves, in particular in my hands, were hurting and any contact made this sensation worse. I had to shift the loop bands from my wrist to my upper arm, as the contact of the bands with my skin was extremely painful.

A dream comes true

The last kilometres of the marathon were an exhilarating experience. I have never used drugs in my life, but the almost unearthly experience of the last 60 to 30 minutes of the race probably comes close to that feeling, I assume. Although my body was about to collapse, mentally I started to get stronger, so close to the finish line. In the final kilometres, I was carried not by my feet, but by my willpower and the thought of the people close to me. Several times I looked at what I had written on my arm before the start of the race: names, catchwords and the countries I had visited, and they provided comfort, focus and energy. I also experienced the excitement of being one of the first two Qataris ever to complete an Ironman race.

As I got closer to the finish line, I saw more athletes starting to walk instead of running, or even worse, fainting. Although I felt sorry for them and knew the massive efforts they had made to come this far, the sight of these men and women spurred me to keep going. The last two kilometres of the race were like a film in slow motion, almost a timeless experience. It was as if I had pushed the pause button on my remote control and the images surrounding me had frozen.

After finishing the last lap, I was finally allowed to take the exit towards the finish line. It was an incredible reward. I had previously passed the same exit seven times. The last 200 metres of the race took an extremely long time, at least in my perception. When my feet felt the red carpet, traditionally laid out to welcome the happy few who complete the Ironman race, I felt like a model on the catwalk, cheered by the crowds.

I still had the strength to jump as I crossed the finish line. In silence, I thanked God for making this possible, realising then that I had only prayed once that day, before starting the race, instead of the usual five daily prayers.

I had done it. I had made my childhood dream come true, although it had taken 28 years of my life. It is almost impossible to describe that feeling: ecstasy, pride and above all gratitude that I was given the possibility to realise my dream. Indeed, anything is possible.

The run: challenges, mistakes and solutions

Challenges	Mistakes	Solutions
• Lost focus (again) after 1.5 hours • Left knee started to ache after 20 km • Nerve pain after 37 km	• Dehydrated (not drinking enough fluids/carbs)	• Drink coke and water to retain energy and focus • Maintain high cadence to limit pain in my knee • Persistence and management

I finished the race in 14 hours and almost 45 minutes. The marathon alone took me about five hours. I could have done better, had it not been for the blackout at the start of the swim. Still, I was quite happy with the result. Most importantly, I had been able to finish, and without major physical problems. My first priority had always been to remain safe and not push myself to the extent that I would endanger my health. It was also a promise I had made to my friends and family.

Despite this, I faced some immediate health problems after finishing. I felt really cold and went to get a massage. The organisation usually offers this to athletes, since muscles are stretched to the limit during the race. On this occasion, the organisers had set up massage facilities in a huge tent. As soon as I lay down on one of the stretchers to get the massage, my head started to spin and I literally felt the blood draining away from it. From the corner of my eye, I observed my friend Ebrahim, who had finished the race in an astonishing 12 hours, 50 minutes and 51 seconds, vomiting, utterly exhausted. I remember my wife talking to me. Maybe she saw what was happening, but could not do anything about it. I fainted. The next thing I remember is being in the aid station. My iron levels were seriously low and I was close to being dehydrated. I was taken from the massage tent to the medical station, where I was given an infusion to rebalance my system for about an hour and a half, while medics tried to revive me by raising my legs and talking to me. I was asked to walk but still felt very dizzy. I had another infusion for about half an hour and the doctors told me they would take me to hospital if I did not feel any better. Luckily I recovered and was allowed to go to the hotel. The strain the Ironman race puts on a human body is immense: 7,000 calories were burned during the race and I lost approximately 2 kilograms in weight.

The run is one of my stronger disciplines, which is not surprising, since I am a small and lightweight athlete. The marathon did not pose the same challenges as the swim. Still, the sensations I experienced while running were diverse and stronger than anything before, even the first 15 minutes of the swim. I had "ups" and "downs," both physically and mentally. Despite starting off well, I lost focus and my body started to protest. Eventually, however, the thrill and excitement which overwhelm you when you realise you will probably cross the finish line, gave me an ecstatic feeling and made me forget my physical pain. In this sense, the last section of the race was probably the most intense. Right at the start, during the swim, I had fallen into a deep hole. However, I ended the race on top of a mountain, with a feeling comparable to mountain climbers when they have finally reached the summit of Mount Everest. And just as I did, those men and women have a tendency to faint close to the top, from lack of oxygen. Unfortunately, there are not yet aid stations on the summit of Mount Everest.

Running a marathon, especially when it is part of an Ironman race, is the ultimate lesson in endurance. It is all about good energy management. Assume that you are the battery of a cell phone, with only 20% power left. How do you manage this throughout the day? Running a marathon can teach us useful lessons for our daily lives. It is all about good preparation, management of time and energy, and persistence. "Whatever you do, don't stop," is what many triathlon coaches advise you. The same goes for what we do at work or at home. It is possible to bring a tedious and complex task or project to an end as long as one remains balanced, persistent and result-oriented ("eyes on the ball").

Chapter 6

The Way Forward

The black hole

After spending a lot of energy working towards a goal and finally achieving it, it is common for people to feel as if they are looking into a black hole, not knowing what to do next. They have lost a sense of purpose. This could have happened to me. What would my purpose in life be, now that I had achieved my objective?

Let me say first of all, that I never let myself be fully consumed by my training. Even when my schedule had become very intense, as in early 2016, I still tried to spend time with my friends and family and have an active social life, although this was not always easy. In this way, I endeavoured not to be controlled by my desire to become an Ironman. Besides, I did not give up my training and exercise altogether after the race, obviously. In the spring of 2017, I participated in Al Samla, in some ways an even more strenuous undertaking than the Ironman race (see box below).

Al Samla

My participation in Al Samla, in April 2017, would almost merit writing another book. Hence, the limited reference to this race does not do it sufficient credit.

Al Samla, which in Arabic refers to challenge, persistence, endurance and patience, is a so-called ultra-endurance race. Only Qatari men aged 18 or older are allowed to take part. It spans 220 kilometres through the Qatari desert and along Qatar's coast and involves several disciplines, including running - the basic discipline - kayaking, mountain biking, swimming and shooting. Shooting is a traditional Qatari sport and has produced one of the few Qatari Olympic medal winners. The race is back-to-back, with a cut-off time of 96 hours.

My friend and Ironman buddy, Ebrahim, convinced me to register for this crazy undertaking and participated himself too. Although "the rabbit" could not finish the race, he would take revenge by giving a great performance at the Half Ironman World Championship, later in 2017. I ended fifth, which would not have been possible without Ebrahim's strong support. I was the oldest athlete finishing in the top 10 and the only one in the top 5 without a military background.

Perhaps you have to be mad to compete in Al Samla. I suffered serious foot injuries and lost several toenails in the race. Still, my Ironman fitness helped me to finish among the best. I am not only referring to my physical condition, although I intensified my training again in the run-up to Al Samla, but also the mental stamina I developed during my journey to become an Ironman.

Sharing experiences

The Ironman race is a very individualistic undertaking, despite the fact that one cannot complete it successfully without the help of others. After finishing, I wanted to share the experience, transforming my individual achievement into a collective asset.

The triathlon's value is often underestimated. It is a multi-faceted sport, demanding endurance, strength and speed. In swimming, the upper body is trained, in biking it is the lower body, and running is cardiovascular exercise. It is a sport that one can do anywhere, even under the sometimes harsh conditions prevalent in my own country. It does not necessarily require expensive facilities.

I have introduced the triathlon to the local community by founding a local club called QTRI (Qatari Triathlon Club) which has continued to grow and now has 120 members. They have been busy learning more about sport and incorporating it into their lifestyle. Many others are preparing for races locally and regionally, and one member succeeded in becoming an Ironman in Australia in May 2017. Not only that: the first, second and sixth positions in the Al Samla race in April 2017 were taken by members of the QTRI group. I also intend to establish a triathlon-training centre, inspired by the training facilities I encountered in Thailand, to be used by the community. I have also been asked to be a board member of the national Cycling and Triathlon Federation (QCTF), in charge of developing the triathlon in the country.

I regularly give motivational talks to community groups, schools and companies and share the experiences of my Ironman journey and the lessons learned from it. This book is another attempt to share these lessons.

Finally, I promote and encourage a healthy lifestyle, especially among Qatari youth. The future lies in their hands. Among them are my nephew Saqer, who felt inspired by my training, and my brother's sons, Hassan and Essa.

Attitudes to sport in Qatar have changed dramatically in the last decade or so, with the realisation that it contributes to national development. National Sport Day was introduced in 2012 and sport is part of the government's National Vision 2030. There has been massive investment in an impressive sports infrastructure, in preparation for the football world championship due to be held in Qatar in 2022. Sport and economic development go hand in hand: the substantial investment in infrastructure has contributed to the country's economic growth and development.

It is also now widely recognised in the country that sport contributes to a healthy lifestyle and can help combat health problems related to the country's prosperity such as obesity and heart disease. The Gulf region has one of the highest rates of diabetes in the world. And with a healthy life style and a healthy body goes a healthy mind. Happiness is not derived from our careers or our car or, in my case, the number of countries we are able to visit. We experience most of our happy moments in life when we are at peace with what we have achieved and are amongst the people for whom we care.

I strongly believe that sharing my experiences can help promote sport in my country and region, as well as a healthy lifestyle and a healthy mind. And by doing so, I hope to contribute to a healthier and more sustainable future.

A sustainable future

The generation of my parents witnessed the country's and region's development from a secluded and remote part of the world to a thriving and wealthy hub between Europe and Asia/Africa. This generation knows what poverty is and realises that results require hard work, discipline and effort.

My generation was raised in relative wealth, but at the same time was very much influenced by the lessons and experience of our parents.

For the younger generation, prosperity is a given and some even regard it as something they are entitled to.

The economic system in our region, founded exclusively on revenues from fossil fuel, may have encouraged this attitude. However, policy-makers in the region have realised that reserves will not last forever, and many countries, including Qatar, have embraced diversification as a cornerstone of economic and social development. Other factors encouraging this trend include the recent low oil and gas price, steps taken by fossil fuel consuming countries to reduce their reliance on these fuels as a source of energy, and internationally agreed targets to reduce emissions from fossil fuel consumption, as part of the fight against global warming and climate change.

Through my work, I hope to contribute to a sustainable future for my country and the region at large. The world around us changes continuously and it is important to adapt. In the 1990s, Nokia was the absolute market leader in cell phones. The company had a remarkable history, as it had started off as a producer of tyres. Despite this, it missed the boat of the smartphone. Or think about the gramophone record, the video and the CD. In the same way, Qatar, now one of the wealthiest countries in the world, faces challenges, and to maintain its current economic and social development, it needs to adapt to changing circumstances. Or put differently, applying a lesson learned from my Ironman experience, it should stay in control instead of being controlled.

Against this background, the University where I work as an adjunct professor has initiated a project, together with a University in Europe, to research conditions that allow for a gradual energy transition, to the benefit of both fossil fuel-consuming and fossil fuel-producing countries and regions.

At the UN Climate Conference in Paris, in December 2015, it was agreed to reduce emissions of CO_2 in order to limit the increase of average temperatures worldwide to 2 degrees Celsius, and preferably 1.5 degrees. If measures to reduce CO_2 emissions are taken very abruptly or very late, requiring substantial interventions, there is a risk they will "strangle" both the economies of fossil fuel- consuming economies as well as those which do not produce fossil fuel. "Turning off the tap" by fossil fuel-consuming countries would seriously hurt economies in the Gulf. A sudden change to renewables would render fossil reserves potentially worthless, producing a "carbon bubble." In fossil fuel-consuming countries, there is a high demand for energy and fossil fuel cannot be substituted easily by renewable energies. An efficient and effective energy transition must be gradual. At the same time, if the Paris climate targets are to be achieved, major investment is necessary in research to increase the efficiency of energy derived from fossil fuel, thereby reducing CO_2 emissions.

Fossil fuel-consuming and producing countries are mutually dependent. If both cooperate, it should be possible to define the conditions which allow oil and gas consuming countries to use fossil energy, while reducing CO_2 emissions, and oil and gas producing countries to continue to extract and sell fossil fuel for a considerable time, while gradually diversifying their economies. One of the ways to cooperate is through joint investments in emission-reducing technologies. The project I have initiated brings together a university in a fossil fuel-producing country and a university in a fossil fuel-consuming country and attempts to integrate the focus of technology and engineering with the focus of economics and finance.

You might ask yourself how this relates to my Ironman journey. The motto of the Ironman competition is "anything is possible." Some people consider our research an attempt to answer the "one million dollar" question. They look at me in disbelief when I tell them. But this challenge is exactly what makes me tick: achieving a goal that appears to be impossible.

To conclude: the importance of...
... dedication, discipline and commitment...

"Be careful what you wish for, you might get it" is a saying with a somewhat negative connotation. In the English language it refers to something that you might not want to get. And "wishing" in itself is not enough. The Latin saying "aut viam inveniam aut faciam" (I shall either find a way or make one) might be a better way to describe my journey to become an Ironman. A childhood dream is an important beginning, but to see it come true requires resolve and discipline.

There is a Spanish saying: "he who wants to eat fish, must get his breeches wet." In his book "Outliers," Malcolm Gladwell tries to explain why some people are very successful in life. Practicing is one of the keys to success. This does not only hold for athletes, but also for business leaders like Bill Gates or Steve Jobs. There appears to be a golden rule: the "great" all trained for at least 10,000 hours in their lives to achieve their ultimate dream. I haven't counted the number of hours I have been training, but I am sure I am getting close.

A good example of this resolve is the story of a friend of mine who decided to study for a PhD. He had the idea in 1993, shortly after he had left university and started his first job. In December 1999, he defended his thesis, although earlier that year he had been very ill and a nearly failed operation took him to the edge of his life. But it did not stop him. He used the time at home recovering from his illness to finish the thesis. In the end, he managed it through hard work and commitment, which was more important than being Albert Einstein, he said. It was not his innate intelligence which won the day. Similarly, in my journey to become an Ironman, I was not outstanding in any of the triathlon disciplines, nor was I particularly physically strong. It was resolve and discipline that finally propelled me past the finish line in South Africa.

It starts with defining your ambition. An ambition can often be inspired by a vision or a dream. Those are the most powerful. Try to state it as concretely as possible. For this purpose, it helps to set targets that are SMART: simple, measurable, ambitious but realistic and bound by time. It helped me to write down my ambitions and targets and reread them from time to time, adjusting them as necessary during my journey. There is nothing wrong with that. On the contrary, it shows that you can adapt to changing circumstances. If the road is blocked, you have to find another way to reach your destination. Or as Jim Rohn once said, "If you really want to do something, you will find a way. If you don't, you will find an excuse."

Another dimension is involving others in your journey. Although becoming an Ironman is a solitary experience, I would not have been able to cross the finish line in Port Elizabeth without the support of many. There is a reason why the acknowledgements of this book are so long. Confide in others and give them your trust, they will definitely support you. And by involving others from the outset, you increase your commitment. There is no way back if they know about your quest.

Having said this, in business or during negotiations it can

sometimes be more effective not to share your goals from the start. In my culture it is quite common not to do so. Being the "underdog", the one nobody is watching, can sometimes be a very effective strategy.

It sounds easy to be dedicated, committed and disciplined. Of course it is not. How to maintain resolve is probably one of the most difficult challenges. Believe me, there have been many moments when I thought about giving up. What helped me to endure?

First, I made a plan and wrote it down. This helped to maintain the discipline of my training schedule. Of course, at times you will have to change your plan, but always keep your ultimate objectives in mind and do not give up on them.

Second, learn from your mistakes. Write them down and periodically re-read the lessons learned. Unfortunately, we live in a world in which making mistakes is not always tolerated. However, we learn from them, not necessarily from our successes. An organisational culture that allows for mistakes, so long as you draw lessons from them and share them, is more effective than one which does not allow for error. As an engineer, I have learned that sharing mistakes and the lessons drawn from them can improve processes and, above all, safety. Mistakes can lead to positive innovations.

Excerpt from my notes, taken during my journey

My learning from triathlon:
- improve my transition time
- prepare and check all gear in advance
- learn to drink while biking, reach bottles while biking
- pace and manage energy while biking

- don't take energy/protein bars during running or biking
- sleep enough prior to race
- do not have a deep massage directly before the race
- do not try new things in the race

Stories
- wrong wet suit
- Forgot goggles on windy and cold day
- running with biking helmet
- mean swim coach
- struggle in open water swim
- miscalculated energy needed for race
- Struggle with pulling zipper before the swim

Professional athletes' tips
- TT bike makes a difference of 20 minutes on 180 km distance
- invest in bike frame then upgrade later, with wheels and gear
- nutrition is very important
- do three half Ironman races before going to full Ironman
- unclip shoes when moving ankle/heel horizontally
- always use rear brake: more stable

Third, do not be consumed by your journey. Lead a balanced life and take sufficient time for recovery, since top athletes can only perform when they take enough time to rest. The same holds for "top athletes" in business or public office. Although healthy nutrition is important, it is sometimes good to "sin" and give yourself a treat. I am a great lover of desserts and good food in general and it helped me to consume sweets occasionally.

Fourth, since the road you travel is long, it helps to set intermediate objectives and celebrate them when they are achieved. Participating in competitions before the race in South Africa were landmarks on my journey. It felt great to have my friends and family around me, cheering and giving praise after the races.

Finally, adopt a "step by step" approach on your journey. A famous mountain climber was once asked how to ascend Mount Everest. He smiled and replied "one step after the other." Divide your journey up into smaller trajectories. When you do this, do not dwell on the distance you still have to travel, but contemplate what you have already achieved.

When you have reached the end of a difficult journey, it will make future ones easier, even though each journey will have unique challenges.

... management and preparation...

For a couple of years, I have been responsible for the technology and development of a national oil company. Innovation and technological developments still interest me. I am also a member of the Board of the Science and Technology Park. In this capacity, I am a member of the jury awarding prizes for the best science projects at high schools. It is always very rewarding to meet students with a passion for science and technology, a rare passion, but so important for the future. Alexander Graham Bell was an inspiring innovator. He was not the inventor of the telephone, as many people think, but the founder of what became one of the largest telecom companies worldwide, AT&T. It was Bell who declared, "before anything else, preparation is the key to success." Benjamin Franklin, one of the founding fathers of the United States, put it like this: "By failing to prepare, you are preparing to fail."

Before the start of the South African Ironman championship, on that early April morning in 2016, my journey, starting in 1988, had been all about preparing myself for this ultimate moment.

Preparation is important, and one cannot do without it for an Ironman race, but it is not enough. You can be very well prepared but still falter at the crucial moment. We have all had these experiences in life. Think about exams we had to take, which we didn't pass because of stress or a sleepless night. Finishing an Ironman race takes something more.

... on-field training

Part of my career was spent in off-shore and on-shore oil and gas fields, working on operations, production, collecting data, analysis and studies. This was important to gain necessary skills and move from a mere awareness of challenges to a level where I can understand and solve them myself. This is what I have done in sport. I execute my plan and do from 8 to 15 hours of training between the disciplines of swimming, biking and running, to master the triathlon and get ready mentally and physically.

... positive thinking and mental strength...

"Being negative only makes a difficult journey more difficult. You may be given a cactus, but you don't have to sit on it." This quote is from a friend and says it all. More important than physical training is the mental strength to get you to the finish. During a race, your body will send all kind of signals telling you to stop. Your muscles will start to ache and ultimately every fibre in your body will be in pain and cry out. There were moments

96

when I was close to surrendering and quitting. At these times you rely on your mental rather than physical strength to enable you to keep going. Four lessons are important.

First, be in control and don't let yourself be controlled by events. True, we can only control life to a certain extent. It is full of uncertainties and risks. Events may overtake us, like serious illness. But even then, we should not allow ourselves to be controlled by it. Life is not the way it is supposed to be sometimes. It is the way it is. The way we cope with it is what makes the difference. I did not let myself be controlled by the waves and current in South Africa, but attempted to control them, or at least control myself.

Second, think positive. When you are thankful for what you have, you are always rewarded with more. Try to stay positive and things will get better. It is like the famous glass, filled halfway with water. Some argue that the glass is half empty, others will claim it is half full. Of course, both are right. But both lines of reasoning reveal completely different attitudes towards life. The optimists among us will always see a glass that is half full. During my journey I encountered many obstacles. I did not get depressed, but tried to find a way around them. When it comes to thinking positive, others can be of great help. It helps to "mirror" your negative thoughts and feelings to somebody else; he or she can help you to put things in perspective and get on track again.

Third, look ahead and not backwards. You cannot start the next chapter of your life if you keep rereading the last one. We learn from mistakes but we should not dwell on them. A friend of mine had some difficulties getting his driver's license. When he made a mistake, for instance not giving priority at a roundabout, his driving instructor told him to "throw the experience on the back seat," and move on to the next roundabout. When you drive, there is not much time to analyse what went wrong. You have to focus on the road and what comes next.

Finally, be patient. "Patience is bitter, but its fruit is sweet," the Greek philosopher Aristotle once said. I experienced this after the Norway marathon. My mistakes meant that it took me about three years to recover from my injuries, but this was a blessing in disguise, since during that time I was forced to stop playing football and was able to focus on preparations for the Ironman race. Patience also helps you pace yourself. In the race, you have to be careful not to peak too early or too late. Patience is a virtue of my culture. It has become extinct in the West, where everything needs to be achieved yesterday.

Shaping our lives

I am convinced that perseverance, preparation and positive thinking can shape our lives in a positive way. True, these lessons are not necessarily a recipe for a successful and happy life. Many things happen in our lives, often beyond our control, that may throw us off course. But especially in those times, the lessons spelled out here may help us to regain control and make the best of our new reality. Never give up, because everything is possible.

Epilogue

Stressed Out
Performed by Twenty One Pilots

I wish I found some better sounds no one's ever heard. I wish I had a better voice that sang some better words. I wish I found some chords in an order that is new. I wish I didn't have to rhyme every time I sang.

I was told when I get older all my fears would shrink. But now, I'm insecure and I care what people think. My name's Blurryface and I care what you think. My name's Blurryface and I care what you think.

Wish we could turn back time, to the good old days. When our momma sang us to sleep, but now we're stressed out. Wish we could turn back time, to the good old days. When our momma sang us to sleep but now we're stressed out.

We're stressed out.

Sometimes a certain smell will take me back to when I was young. How come I'm never able to identify where it's coming from? I'd make a candle out of it if I ever found it. Try to sell it, never sell out of it, I'd probably only sell one.

It'd be to my brother, 'cause we have the same nose. Same clothes homegrown a stone's throw from a creek we used to roam. But it would remind us of when nothing really mattered. Out of student loans and tree-house homes we all would take the latter.

We used to play pretend, give each other different names. We would build a rocket ship and then we'd fly it far away. Used to dream of outer space but now they're laughing at our face. Saying, "Wake up, you need to make money" Yeah.

Stressed out

When I first heard this song, performed by Twenty One Pilots, I felt as if it had been written for me. When we are young, we envy the lives of grown-ups. But only when we have achieved maturity and lost our innocence, do we realise that our youth was probably the most carefree time of our lives. "You will only see it when you understand it," my football hero Johan Cruyff once said.

When we mature, there appears to be little room for dreams, fantasy or creativity. We are supposed to meet the expectations of our society: get a good education, marry and raise a family, get a good job that allows us to make money and earns us respect and a good reputation. If we do not succeed, society rejects us. We envy our neighbours who have a larger house or car, or can go on holiday to more luxurious resorts than we do. We envy our colleagues who are promoted. Being good at the game of office politics becomes the key to success. Materialism has become our idol and we forget that true joy comes from the simple things in life. We are all like little rats on a treadmill, going nowhere and just running until the day we die. "Wake up, you need to make money."

Luckily people are realising that this ought not to be the purpose of our life. In particular the younger generation seems to be more enlightened. Life is very short. According to scientists, the universe is almost 14 billion years old. Now assume that the life span of an average human being is about 80 years. Put another way, if the universe was 80 years old, the life span of a human being would be approximately 0.02 seconds. That's nothing. If life is so short, let's try to make the most of it and leave this world having made it a little bit better than when we arrived, which is quite a challenge in 0.02 seconds. Let's not forget our childhood dreams or our great ambitions, let's try to make them come true.

I had a childhood dream to become an Ironman and I achieved it. I also realised that the lessons I learned on the journey can be applied to achieving any dream. Nothing is impossible.

From a dream to a practical tool

A dream written down with a date becomes a goal. A goal broken down into steps becomes a plan. A plan backed by actions makes your dream come true.

In many organisations, people feel constantly under pressure with workloads increasing and no clear priorities. Focus is often lacking. People are very busy, but at the end of the day they have often not achieved anything. A lot of time and energy is spent on internal stakeholder management and turf fights. And despite all the efforts of management to write and communicate business plans, performance targets and key performance indicators, people are not happy and not clear about what to do. So how can lessons learned through the Ironman experience help here?

First, write down what exactly you want to achieve in, let's say the next six months, how you want to do it and when you will reach the finish line. As you are moving towards your goals, write down challenges, mistakes that were made and solutions that were found.

Remember three important things.

First, you are fully responsible for achieving these goals. You are the owner, nobody else. You are the one who will have to finish the swim, the bike ride and the run. So no more pointing fingers to others or hiding in the closet, no more "buts." The targets have to be formulated in such a way that it is clear it is your own responsibility.

Second, you still need other people to support you in reaching these targets. They could be your manager, a colleague or a friend. They are like Joseph, my other coaches, mentors and those I met and trained with, who have more experience. They do not take over. Joseph did not do the South African Ironman Championship. He helped me to cross the finish line by providing help and support. Ask for feedback continually and thank people for it. If other priorities come up during the six month period, which cannot always be avoided, consult your "coach" to decide which task should be done first. But there should be no more than three "disciplines" to complete successfully during this period. Of course, this doesn't imply that you should not do other things during this half year. But you need to focus on three predefined goals.

Third, after each six-month period, there should be an evaluation to assess whether you have achieved your targets and to share challenges, mistakes and solutions. These should be shared with your mentor who can help you with your questions and doubts and with your colleagues, allowing everybody to learn in the process. At the same time, you formulate three new priorities for the next six months and the process starts all over again.

Arithmetic teaches us that by applying the above

methodology, the effectiveness of an organisation increases dramatically. Assume that a division or department consists of 100 people: 100 times three (goals) times two (half years) implies the achievement of 600 targets in a year. Of course, not all of them will be realised. And the achievement of some goals requires a longer period than six months. But still, this practical tool allows an organisation to be more result-oriented, more focused and ultimately do more than previously.

You might argue that this methodology works in a professional environment but is not applicable to private life. I would contest that. I followed the process outlined above in the field of amateur sport. My good friend who became seriously ill while writing his PhD thesis used the same formula to get his illness under control. However, you will need to find at least one "coach" - a friend, your partner in life, a family member, etc. - who is willing to support you and is as committed as you are to helping you achieve your goals.

When it concerns your personal life, it is always good to share the lessons learned during your journey after you have crossed the finish line. Maybe these lessons will provide relief, support or even consolation to others. And maybe you will then add a little bit of value to the world during your 0.02 seconds on earth. "Wake up – and swim, bike and run!"

The skyline of Doha's West Bay in 2017. The country has embraced modernity and rapid economic development, which has made it one of the most affluent countries in the world.

Football was and still is the love of my sport life. This picture was taken at the high school tournament in Doha. I am the boy wearing all white outfit, who has just been tackled. My team came out second, despite being the underdog of the tournament.

The cover of my favourite book when I was a kid, an atlas. I used to study the maps and the world's geography, imagining I was a pilot going to foreign lands in my spaceship I sometimes fell asleep with my head on the book.

Tromso, Norway (June 2011), having finished the Midnight Sun Marathon.
A blissful moment, but the start of a period with multiple injuries.

Triathlon at The Pearl, Doha (March 2015): the "rabbit", the "lion" and the "turtle".

The Doha TriClub. I am proud to call them my friends. All of them were an inspiration, and training with them has helped me to stretch my limits.

Training camp in Thailand, Thanyapura in Phuket (July 2015). The great facilities I encountered there inspired me to establish similar ones in Qatar.

Finishing my first half Ironman, December 2015 in Bahrain. At that time I did not contemplate participating in a full Ironman race, only five months later.

The Dubai half Ironman race (January 2016), with my friend Ibrahim Al-Romaihi (the "rabbit"). We would be the first Qataris to finish a full Ironman race.

With Syafei and Ebrahim, having fun together after our long training at Dukhan prior to the South Africa Ironman race.

With my friends at the ITU World Triathlon Series, Abu Dhabi (2016). One of my last races to prepare for the Ironman race in South Africa. Indeed, "no excuses".

In my hotel room in Port Elizabeth, before the start of the Ironman race. Good preparation is everything.

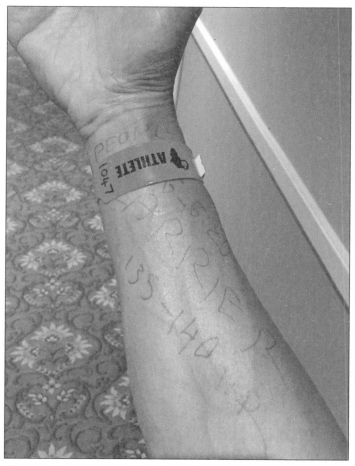

These scribbles on my arm helped me to focus during the Ironman race.

10th April 2016: dawn in Port Elizabeth, South Africa. The start of the Ironman African Championship. Athletes finding their way into the Indian Ocean for a 3.8 kilometre swim.

The transition from swimming to biking in South Africa. I had just completed one of the most difficult swims in my triathlon career.

Biking in the streets of Port Elizabeth, a huge relief after my adventure in the Indian Ocean.

Sunset at the Ironman African Championship and running the marathon. A strong mind kept me going.

The first ever from my country at my age group to finish a full Ironman race. Notice the bracelets I am wearing high up my arms as I could not bear to have them on my wrists, due to nerve pain.

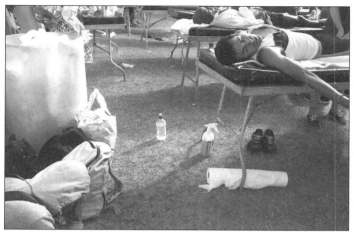

After we finished the full Ironman race, we passed out, suffering from dehydration and fatigue. Still, I would not have wanted to miss the experience of crossing the finish line. The mind can be stronger than the body.

A childhood dream coming true. This medal represents the journey I made to achieve this dream. I dedicate it to all the people who have helped me turn my dream into reality.

Members of the QTRI (Qatari Triathlon Club) club participating at a local triathlon, sprint distance.

My nephews taking part in a local triathlon race.

At the start line with QTRI (Qatari Triathlon Club) members taking part in the local Al Samla 220 km race, April 2017.

Me at the finish line of the Al Samla 2017 race, reaching 5th place overall, welcomed by family members and media.

Celebrating with a large group of local participants and the president of the National Cycling and Triathlon Federation after the MIA race, January 2017.

Giving a motivational talk to Aspire students, April 2017, sharing the experiences of my Ironman journey and the lessons learned from it. This is one of many talks I have given to community groups.

الاجتماع الاول لفريق كيوتراي QTRI للعبة الثلاثية في قطر

The first committee meeting of the QTRI, July 2017, with committee members and myself as founding president.

As a board member of the National Cycling and Triathlon Federation (QCTF) and in charge of developing the triathlon in the country, I attended the annual ITU congress in the Netherlands, Sept 2017, representing the country and registering it at the International Triathlon Federation.